Amused

to

Death

by Eric T. Shortridge

For information contact :
LandonsCry@gmail.com
www.LandonsCry.com

Cover design by Rynda Shortridge-Seckel

First Edition: Oct 2019

Titles available from author

Landon's Cry

Follow the Leader

The last words of a dying muse

available in paperback and digitally online where great books
are sold

Table of Contents

the matador's cape
Once again
Cicerone
the morning of winter's water
terminal
requests
sweet dreams
only the frames remain
Time's windowsill
foolish games
glossy eyes
Now
crematory ashes in November's wind
apocalypse now
Half past 10
the Screenplay
two parts, half full
frayed
here I am
it's time
burnt wax with vanilla red
thank you sir, may I have another?
sad but true
Take care
the auction
please wipe your feet, before stepping on me
don't blink
when angels scream
exhumed
floating
the mark of a question
may I have this last dance?
dreams imprisoned in grey matter
solitaire
negative energy
Suicidal turtles

sleepy dreams
the attic stairs
do you know your enemy?
Diary of a mad man
I never promised you a rose garden
the screams from dandelion kisses
motel 666
null and void
hieroglyphical mirages
When your eyes were tiger striped
Illusions
flavors of ash
my grave marker
the sound of you
the sound of me
shipwrecked
7, 8, lay them straight
shatter and thyme
day old hate
weeping statues
Torn
tis the season
shadows luck between karma and fate
empty chambers
falling backwards
so cold it burns
again and again
somewhere inside the shadow
forsaken
Breaking down
running through closed doors
ready, aim...
running in circles
singing over winter's grave
Nature's Shakespearean play
magically delicious

haiku hiccups
Time
chess
the river
heaven scent
elusive
blessed are the poor
What if
Spring time
my favorite song
the sound of autumn falls
Yesterday
Victoria's secret
Dear Michael,
I beg to differ
Mother Goose
paper rocks and broken scissors
pruning
divided we fall
ivory poachers
take two of these and call me in the morning
the machine
staring at the sun
the patients are running the asylum
I support publick educashion
give peace a chance
talking in my sleep
when the tornado passes
buckle up
unexpected hunger pains
Poker face
programmable
wake me up when it's over
kicking cans
It's a game
I want a refund

Numbers
Doctrines of Darkness
360
thou shall beat him with the rod
the blind hitch hiker
Across the desert
hypocrisy
family reunion
dead mens bones
bitter sweet
Fire and Ice
when doves cry
the awakening
it just hit me
sweet dreams
Emergency
Darwin's theory
the Georgia guidestones
in through the out door
storm chasers
the four seasons
the absence of shadow
Overcome
hidden, but never lost
dragons in the canyon
When angels are born
fear of the dark
the wayside
elevator music
wide awake
unknown
last night
next stop
the shadow of man
magical forest
Ya'll come bak nah ya hear

bobbing for apples
The Watering Hole
new and improved ravings of a stark-naked mind
weeping willows
a glutton for punishment
the god called Law
behind enemy lines
winter ice
you blew your kisses, like candles in the wind
chaotic autumn sleeves
statues
death, on piano
Memories Whisper Through the Mist of Pain
Snowflakes Fall Upon the Painted Frozen Desert
The Scent of Remembrance Floats Through the Air
a mile in my shoes
Misery loves company
listening to the wind
tears and rain

the more I know

I know I don't belong

the cardboard boxes the world tried to put me in
suffocated me
the night was long
and bitter tight
longer than the chains
stronger than its bite
but I emerged in the dawn
to find my soul waiting for me

Who placed me upon this earth?
in this body?
in this time?
why?
the why became longer than any question I could answer

Is there a path for me
already laid?
do I dare go off track?
can I ever go back?

I don't have the voice
to join in this world's choir
they're better off without me
but the line's been drawn
we are all
a piece of this community puzzle

I don't belong here
I can't conform to society
can we all agree
that none of us think exactly alike

can we all just be
free
live and let live

so if you feel like you don't belong
if your voice is too high for this world to hear
then take my hand
and let's sing together
my friend
we'll build a train
stopping this reign of terror and war
coming down
we'll lift our heads up
scream truth upon the housetops
we'll live to see a heaven upon earth
as it was always meant to be

You're not alone
I see you
standing there
right beside me
true poetry
giving yourself permission
to question
everything

we'll search for the truth
throwing everything we've learned away
time to start over
it's not time to roll over
the madness can be put away
if we demand change
releasing the doves
that have been caged in the capitals of the world

I know I don't belong
I didn't build this world
too quick to judge
and too blind to see
but the winds of change
I see a train coming
I see you
and I see me
You're not alone in this sea
Can you hear me?

It's time that we all
grab a hold of this wheel
and steer it off course
to a future not yet seen

Peace

the sundial

September's child held Virgo's breath
waiting to be born
but October brought November's pain
December's rain became the Nile
and all its hope was swept down January's river in swaddling
clothes
the ground was hardened from 28 days of hard labor
but the seed
plowed into March
April prayed mother May I
while the guilt from June hung
around the neck of July
August remembered the mercy of Leo and the promise of a
child
which would save the world
so September holds the Virgin's breath
with Gemini's grip
holding a scarlet thread
waiting for the chaos to end

Monday fights over Tuesday's morsel
and no one rests on the Sabbath anymore
but quietly
between the noise
and static
a secret was born
as the seeds had been planted
watered by invisible flowers, the vine from heaven grew
fragrant

the Poetry was streaming through St. Peters gate
and everyone upon earth with ears
began to see the light

The sun spelled truth upon the moon's dark side
and the lies and deceit
could no longer hide
as every mountain shook
for the mustard seeds
had finally taken root

the last dandelion

the gravity from tomorrow's inhale
weighed
atlas weakened

yesterday's exhale
left me wanting
swimming in quicksand and regret

so I hold my breath

I offered a pound of flesh
but Father time raised the stakes

I told my brother
I told my sister
to look upon my palms
and side
tried to place their hands inside
but they were blind
they were looking
behind
memorizing the passages of time
King James style

so I hold my breath

my hair grew crippled
as the nightmares were told
every night at bed time
the most trusted news source
planted a seed in my head
wrapped in lies and silken sheets
telling the world what's planned ahead

the day before yesterday
filmed in black and white footage
fast forward to the wrinkled voices of war
trembling
the day after tomorrow
the bombs drop in color
and stereo

I told my neighbor
we need to look out for each other
told my enemy
I forgive you
but they were deaf
their souls
desensitized
their hearts cold
their minds washed
skin calloused
imprisoned
I showed them the key
but they could not understand me

so I held my breath
until the red died with blue
then blew my wish
and bid adieu

Secrets of the grandfather clock

I was only seven
when I said tomorrow
I'm going to draw heaven
for my mother

but tomorrow never came
the alarm never rang

I was only eleven
the first time
I saw a homeless man begging
I said tomorrow
I'll come back
but he died later that night
Today never comes
it's always a day too late

I was nineteen
when I stamped that Fathers day card
that was never sent
for today
was the last day
signed and sealed
but never delivered
crying for days afterward
my hand frozen in pall bearers grip

Capitalism demanded my attention
eight hour a day marathon
daylight savings time
gave me an extra hour of insomnia

twenty-four
when I signed the divorce paper
a single father
raising a little daughter
tomorrow was dragged into next year
today was over too soon
yesterday
the tassels flew
Teaching a baby bird
what to do
and what not to
the predators and traps lying in wait
regurgitating life's lessons
trying to get the baby to chew
and swallow
to be bold
to be different
to follow the heart

imparting the last remnants from wisdoms gut
I learned to remove the tentacles of procrastination
learned that today
is all we have
and to never wait for tomorrow

in the end
what have we got to lose?

Time
it's not on your side

the left over glue from post-it notes

The fairy dust
was clumped and moldy
stuffed in yesterday's drawer
waiting for tomorrow
to come out just as planned

my libraries
filled with diaries
couldn't be insured
so I didn't burn
these pages stained
when my heart bled dry

I was hoping for one more day
never see that rope fray
when night is day and all you can see
is your horoscope in the sky
living a lie

I chewed the placenta
coughed on air
I didn't belong here
I wanted to go back home
where everything is warm
and the memories sing and dance
play in the rain
skip rope to a sun that never sets

I came, I saw, and life kicked my ass
tried to keep me down
so I threw imagination upon my own canvas
sunk the pen deeper into possibilities
tattooed over the nightmares

took off my shirt
and let everyone see
the bruising

I stood up while time was slipping
went skinny dipping
didn't see you at first
behind the red brush
your limbs so tender and fragile
but your will was stronger than ever

swimming upstream
I heard your scream
and I heard your whisper
the beach was littered
with the stains of gossip from secrets gone public
the stench tried to follow us
so we both held our breath
and swam deeper

books were speaking
and our lips poured the most delicate of wine
resting upon the isle of epiphany
we saw tomorrow wasn't coming
and that's when
we reached for each other
with nothing to lose
our lips became the softness of the sky

the dust and water
began mixing together
we carved our initials with leftover fairy dust
"we were here"

a note from today
written for a tomorrow that never came

my tattered kite

Snowflakes whisper upon the painted frozen desert
I cast my kite upon memories wind
Higher and younger I become in the distance

An adult, regret and responsibilities
higher and higher
A teenager, hopes and dreams
higher and higher
A child, fun and games

Suddenly my kite rips through the clouds
As realities lightning strikes
And the string is lost

As a skydiver without a parachute,
Suddenly the ground is before me
And my dreams are smashed within

I wish to travel backwards,
But my kite will not take me

Too tired for games, and too wise to hope
I carry my tattered kite
Because in my dreams, it still flies
Please, do not wake me

Loved, to death

Tied
to one post
Chained
between two testaments
unable to move to solid ground
pound
the crashes sound

the water smashing
crashing
baptizing
flooding the ground of her fertile mind
pound
pound
as the nails are driven in

the keys to freedom
escaped her memory
she had held them once
upon a time
there lived a young girl
love was her life
truth her god
carrying innocence in her eyes
but, now
as the storm brews upon the seashore
the moon is full tonight
the dry landmark is ten feet above
waking up chained
was it all a dream?

was I ever free?
and when did I let my enemy enslave me

when did I stop believing?
when did I stop seeking?

in the sea of Babylon
upon dying knees
the lightning crashes her awake
pound
pound
pound

someone is knocking on the door

it was all a bad dream

bolding standing in the sunlight
now
she vows
never again to fall asleep
with arms wide open

rubbing her raw wrists
with handcuffed indentions
she watches the scabs slowly heal
every good intention

No trespassing

Found myself ~ waking up
in the middle of a pig sty
but the welcome mat read
Home sweet home

wondering why then remembering how
I bowed my head and eyes
and lifted 21 grams into the skies
seeking
forgiveness came quickly
and the warm breeze stayed with me

but I had my own cross to bear
and the verdict read guilty
my voice hammered steel sins
the past cried out
"Crucify!"

but then a voice next to me
said crisply
"Truthfully
Die already
then Rise
and walk with me"

The Sacrifice

forty days without food or water
the desert burning Summer's late arrival
everything became a blur
just as the devil
appeared as a mirage

holding a pitcher of iced tea
and some kind of deliciousness
upon a plate
overflowing with a field's bounty

I watched in a daze
through the humid haze
my mouth coated in cotton
the plate was calling my name

He sat next to me
I stared

throwing three nails into the dust
He said I could trust
everything he said
"Make a wish"
The serpent's tongue flickered

"I want to eat
I want to drink
then share them with the hungry and thirsty;
the humble and meek"

"Two wishes... two nails"
the snake slithered

Only one nail remained
one last wish to gain

"Eternal Life"
But before I spoke
I counted the cost

"Your wish is my command"

So he took the three nails
then nailed my feet and hands

in memory

Sun rising
Mind dreaming
Brain sleeping
Alarm ringing
Oversleeping
Uniform changing
Wreck less driving
Time clock punching
Coffee drinking
Lobby filling
Client complaining
Surgery waiting
Start Sedating
Tumor removing
Spay and Neutering
Head shaking
Hematoma forming
Shepherd coughing
Heartworm checking
Poodle scratching
Cortisone injecting
Possible poisoning
Leukemia testing
Three days vomiting
Not eating or drinking
Blood drawing
Patient escaping
Dog shearing
Fangs baring
Cat bathing
Cat freaking
Cat scratching
Arms bleeding

Lunchtime heeding
No time for eating
Bathroom hiding

Help calling
Stretcher carrying
Car hitting
Dog dying
Quick examining
Brain swelling
Pupils constricting
Gums paling
Shallow breathing
Catheter inserting
Everyone moving
Stethoscope listening
Thoughts racing
Brow sweating
Endo-tracheal tubing
Keep working
Oxygen pumping
Keep hoping
Manual breathing
Keep trying
Blood losing
Meds failing
Beat slowing
Life fading
People screaming
Hearts breaking
Paws twitching
Head lowering
Apologizing
Monitor flat lining
Eyes closing
Brain sleeping

Heavenly dreaming

Red Sea parting
And suddenly
Everyone sees the little girl
Who had been hidden behind the veil of commotion
Can't recall what she was wearing
Hugging her Barbie so very tightly
Just remember the pain and anguish written upon her face
And the tears streaming down her trembling lips
Her entire being shaking
Reaching a tiny quivering hand
Lightly upon her pet's head
Gently petting her best friend
Under her choking sobs, she cries
"Wake up Buddy...
Wake up!
Wake up!
Daddy, he won't wake up"

Her father breaks down
Hugging his daughter so very tightly
Carrying her away
Leaving a river trailing behind
And a memory not soon forgotten
Sun setting
Darkness falls

I shook my head

There came a knock on the door
sounding a bit different
different than before

it was the knock of a king
and everything became crystal
when the voice rang

He said "I've got something"

that's when I opened my eyes
that's when I looked around
seeing the dirty sound
the mess
I was living in
I didn't want to let him in
not in the state my house was in
but the pounding continued
so I opened the door and let him in

I kind of
snuck
into a corner's shadow
apologized
for the condition my home was in
I said sorry for this
and sorry for that
sorry I didn't clean the welcome mat

then he said something
something I didn't expect

He said, "You called me
You cried out
it was You - that sought me out"

He said,
"I've got something for you"

handed me a letter
with my name on it

smiling and walking away
the scent of forgiveness
still lingering in the air

I tore open the envelope
to find a mystery - I read a riddle
written from hell

I shook my head
and found the epiphany inside a mustard seed shell

The answer
to
a
prayer

The last door on the left

Everything was upside down
I turned the sky into ground
then made it mine
stopping the hands of time
changed the air into stairs
I began my ascent

faith can't move mountains
it just helps you climb them
my Everest was called Mt. Fear
and I dug in there
for the long night

Soon everything became quiet
everything became black
the atmosphere held its breath
thick
the fog slept across my back
my nerves were stretching further
so I pretended they were steel

I could not see the fangs
until I felt them
in my neck
but I knew whose they were
as I swung my ice pick
through its heart

behind eyes of angels
I saw the beast, dead at my feet

a shepherd approached me

I said, 'thank you
for giving me the strength'

He placed his hand upon my head
"*No,*
my child...
It was You"

the dream exploded as my spirit fell back down
the sun arose as Father Time tapped his watch
my heart skipped a beat
The world was upside down
because I
I was upside down
I was daydreaming
I was dying

watching these moments filling my mind
these last flickering flashes of time
the last drink from this canteen
savoring every drop

I needed everything to make sense
but it all just melted as day became night
as everything became quiet
everything became black
and the blanket
grew cold

I held my breath
closed my eyes

and hoped for the best

Reflections of déjà vu

I held a beating heart in the palm my hand
but it crumbled in the end
holding on too tight
for fear of letting go
splintered years collapsed in slow motion

I pressed the pause button
with every tear that dropped into the abyss
my eyes enveloped the wings of red panic
and behind them
the blinking walls became my tomb

In the darkness
is when the movie played
over and over again
the last grain of sand
between the cracks of my hand
the dead color fell from Autumn's torn dress

The cold slithered in with the night
before I could seek
refuge
before I could pray
everything precious lie buried under midnight's broken hand
and beneath the quicksand
Abel's brother screamed murder

The angels had fallen with Winter's moon
but their faces remained righteous
as they built a snowman
my soul frozen

the icicles tasted like cherry wood
stakes
hemorrhaging
the blood was cold
but it was my own
I cried out to the heavens
my words stumbling
The ice was cracking
the angels were laughing

The god of Hades flashed a flaming knife
and wrote my name in marrow and ash
dipping its fingers into my arteries and veins
it painted a future in black crystal balls

but then a guiding light
pierced the igloo
and I knew
everything would be alright
as lightning it crashed
and my halo burned bright
the shadow creatures convulsed when the trumpet sounded
they tried to hide as the mountains fell
the silence of Love
consumed them all
the keeper of the beating heart
smashed my prison in the palm of His hand
and in slow motion
the light consumed the night
Beelzebub's tongue filled my lungs with dead earth
but in the end
I knew everything would be alright
for the keeper of the beating heart
had become my guiding Light

granite paper shaped scissors

The will to survive fought to see the light of day
rising with the sun
running behind the wind
sharpening instincts sword
the third eye blinked
twice
surveying the land
my heart shook its hand
as the body shook its head

I opened my mouth to find a white flag
lying just under my tongue
a morsel of promise in a stale fortune cookie

the blood that swam through my veins screamed
never
the battlefield
had spread to the mind's river
the flesh had retreated
leaving no evidence behind

the bright city nights had crept into the fertile lands
homo sapiens spread the news like wildfire
leaving disease in its wake of corruption
industrial pollution
but hope
and faith
had learned to adapt
evolve
hiding inside the roots, they fed those who were seeking
hibernation was not an option

the storm came by manual operation
the sounds of war
whispered dust on fallen leaves

out of the forest
a voice beckoned
me
falling to one knee
I heard the tree fall
and in the midst of it all
peace rolled its cotton carpet upon the floor
allowing the door
to be seen

the handle was gold and green
silk spinning
my spirit began breathing
a light not its own

the window of my soul
pierced the atmosphere
my eyes drew stars behind the gray lining
and every thought
became everything
for infinity

and the will to live
survived another day

I quit

I tried on your friends
found myself too big
and even the most expensive champagne
could not erase the lingering aftertaste
of your sacred opinion
sugared with artificial saccharine

behind the disguise
the truth always finds the fakery
you tried to hide your loftiness behind an elephant

you took the title you never deserved
wrapped it all inside of you
trying to build your own kingdom
upon the backs of those you despise

the suffering continues
only money makes the bleeding stop
turning away those who have never held
Benjamin Franklin's hand

management climbed the social ladder
dangling a suicide noose in every hotel room
a bible in the sock drawer

it was your laugh
that gave you away
your smile twinkled crooked with delight
white teeth masking a bleached conscious

the mask of greed found you a perfect fit

all bow to the face of Pharaoh

sticks and stones

Four Eyes
Idiot
Fatso
Cry baby
Ugly
Faggot
Whore
Moron
Scumbag
DoucheBag
Weirdo
Freak
Loser
Dog
Slut
Pig
Virgin
Lesbian
Queer
Shall I go down the list?
StupidBitch
CockSucker
DumbMotherFucker

Sticks and Stones
Your words did more than hurt me
They killed me
Buried in a rubble of rock
A stick cross - my grave marker
Crucified all over again

But in the end
The joke is on you
For I am your Maker

It's too bad you could not see my heart
It is too sad you could not see past my skin
Because I was Jesus Christ within
The one who died for your sin
Remember Me?

And you thought I was no longer here
Thinking I was somewhere up there
I've been here all along

I gave you an opportunity
A chance for all eternity
For you - To touch Me
For you - To see Me
For you - To know Me

Facebook Faker
Every day church goer
Self righteous Holy Roller
Angels call YOU the Joker

Don't pretend to raise your hands towards Me
Higher you lift them into the sky
All the while, I'm sitting right behind you
And you can't even look me in the eye

Do you remember that list?
Cause I'm like the real Santa
The true giver of gifts
And I am also keeping a list

I was starving for love
Thirsty for a hug
I was in prison
And you walked away
With a bible tucked under your arm
Wearing a shirt labeled WWJD
And you say you see?
Heartless and blind
Damning those around you
But now the other shoe
Is suddenly upon you

Yes, I am keeping a list
The words from your own lips

black eyes and nails

Born with a black eye
they called it genetic
before the seed could be planted
the fig leaves had already been plucked

Learning to walk
on this tightrope
between fate and luck
between heaven and hell
rolling the dice of infinity
Learning to talk
whisper and yell
holding one nail

and then two nails
and finally
three

The truth was screaming
to be set free
to be found
I started seeking
but couldn't see ahead
to where the voices led
and that's when they found me
stopped me
placed another nail in my head
and some words
we think he said

the darkness crept in with the shadows of yesterday

and then the questioning

blasphemer

unbeliever

die a sinner

they told me this black eye
was genetic
nothing could erase it
found
it
to be black lipstick
found religion kissing my neck
bleeding the truth like a leech

found the vampire bats
hiding
inside the tower and steeple
the pied piper was calling all the children
but the voice of wisdom
held a key
larger than any book

I began to see
when I finally found the hammer
and nailed myself free

walking through the pages

Walking through this world of pages
Seeking truth through all the ages
I find a tree and hide under its shade
I examine the leaves
taste its fruit
My mouth becomes bitter

Another tree I find, I play in its branches
Until a snake comes along, and whispers in my ear
"Believe me"
I look in its mouth
darkness rotting
speaking in tongues
of religion

So I walk through the pages
Seeking truth through all the ages
Sudden feet have come upon me,
Rocks begin to rain down
Cast from those who traded truth for lies
Blindly they throw
yet those rocks find the mark
Pelted again
bruised again
bloodied again
Broken again…
I limp through the pages
Seeking truth through all the ages

Hungry and thirsty
I see a glimmer of water
So I quicken my pace

The closer I get… the louder they get
"You're a sinner and God hates sin!"
Dressed in black they encircle me
Their words like sticks beat me down
Their screams as bricks wear me down
I now see the water is stagnant
carcasses surrounding
I shield my heart and walk right through them
crawling through the pages…
Seeking truth through all the ages

The desert heat is stifling
No shade from this burning
No comfort for my mourning
No dressing to heal my wounds
Only my desire to search through all these pages
Seeking truth, somewhere through the ages
It is only this desire now, that keeps me going
Like some animal instinct
Like a salmon returning to where it was born
I will find my destination or die trying
A soft breeze begins to blow
While the vultures above begin to crow
Skeletons all around me
I can no longer see my feet beneath me
Sinking in quicksand
Is this my fate, how I should die

But just then a hand reaches down
a voice whispers from above
"My friend, where have you been?"

With dry mouth and cracked lips,
"I've been walking through all these pages
Seeking truth through all the ages"

And now as I stand upon my feet
The stranger now gone,
I hear a voice roll like thunder…

"Tear through all the pages…
and behold the truth that still rages"
Tear through all the pages

so I tore through all the pages
finding rest beyond the ages

To my guardian angel

Dear Guardian angel,

Where were you
when I made that terrible mistake?
No, not that one
The other one
Were you sleeping on the job?

Where were you, when I went chasing after demons?
Were you taking a lunch break?

And those one-night stands
Why didn't you just stop me?
Or did you just sit and watch me
Did you tattle on me?

Guardian angel
How do you like the movie so far?
Does it get boring when I sleep?
Or do you follow me
Even in my dreams
Maybe you're the one who wakes me
During my nightmares
Never thought of that before

When I flipped my car several times over
I thought you would have stopped it
But in the end
I guess you're the one who breathed for me

And that time when I fell asleep at the wheel
Thank you for waking me up

Just in time

So thank you guardian angel, for keeping me alive
And sorry for the guilt trip
just remember...
I haven't received my wings yet

I was kind of hoping that you would have stopped me from
making so many mistakes
But I guess that's my job

I would like to know your name and see your face
But not quite ready, to cross those pearly gates

So Guardian angel...
Just one request please
When death comes calling my name
Fight for me
Tell the Reaper, 'Not now'
I promise that I will fight beside you

But dear Guardian angel
When it is my time to go
I understand
But before my spirit drifts away
Promise me
That you will play the violin for me

Postcards from Patmos

the citizens of Babylon
built a tower
they said the end of the world was near
so they built a steeple
reaching up to the heavens

God saw the confusion
how each tribe
had their own language
one thousand denominations

The Egyptians built the pyramids
in honor of their Trinity
the people wanted a king

The Greeks came upon the battle scene
with the philosophy of Aristotle and Socrates
more questions than answers
Alexander
gave us Hades

the Romans ruled the world
with an iron fist
Jerusalem was looking for a savior
with an iron fist

they said the end is near
and a savior did appear
he said he came to die for our sins
but they wanted a king

Nero played the fiddle
as the blood of Abel cried
Constantine had a vision
started mixing religion
the Romans suddenly became Holy
as the Emperor donned a funny hat

the Pope ruled from a city within Rome
began selling indulgences
money for your soul
back then
the offering plate came with teeth
and the priests ruled the night
the clouds of Revelation began to part

Martin Luther had visions of Nostradamus
"the anti christ is now with us"
666
the 'Vicar of Christ' in Greek
written upon the head
of this beast
they said the end was here
so very near

the church hid the bible from peasant eyes
while roasting the heretics alive

the dragon reared its 7 heads in the absence of light
the dark ages swallowed the flesh and blood
of innocent men, women, and children
placed inside the Iron Maiden
confess
confess
confess
the demons of the apocalypse
stretched ligaments and sinew

pulling every joint out of place
put you back together, just to do it all over again
then came the plague
the guillotine followed
and they all began looking for a savior
to return
they had forgotten
that he already came
they couldn't remember why he came
He said he came to die for our sins
and if you seek me
you shall find me

two thousand twenty
and everyone is looking for a savior to return
but He already came
He came to do
what He sought out to do
and it was Perfect
but today
that isn't enough
because we no longer cry for a savior
we want a king
when will we learn
the savior we're waiting for
already came

heaven isn't above
it's right here below
hell isn't below
it's right here above

stop looking for a future king
It's in our spirit that He reigns

pass the mustard, please...

I dropped my cross
as the world became too heavy to bare
I'm sorry Lord
I'm coming home
with no gifts to bare

I dropped my halo
then swept it under the rug
somewhere along the line
it became broken
and all the rubbing
never made it rise again

I dropped my money
into the offering plate
but the blessing never came my way
seemed it did a U turn
blessing the pastor
with a brand new car

I dropped the book
they said you wrote for me
as I found too many things
that just couldn't be

I dropped my sword
as it only cut those around me
dropped the shield and helmet
that never did protect me

I dropped my head
dropped my pride as I realized
I'll remain a sinner until I die

I dropped religion
though it begged me not to go
and I imagined
there were no wars

I'm dropping the mask
nothing left to hide

standing naked and bare
still holding this mustard seed
I'm dropping it now
won't you water it

please

hush little baby

Broken glass, shards of glass
Walking over broken glass
Picking up the pieces
Shattered hopes
Broken dreams
Bloody broken pieces

I've become the rock upon the floor
The stone which broke the windows of my soul
Cast by the one I love

Bloody footprints mark the floor
Following your boots outside the door
Broken glass
Shards of glass
Picking up the pieces
No one sees my bloody feet
A smile hides the broken heart
This rock you've thrown
Covered in lies
Woven in deceit
Slippery from your spit
Treat your mother like a toilet
With bleeding eyes
And pleading cries
I begged you not to go

My only child
Become the broken glass beneath my feet
Open scabs upon calloused knees
Praying God help me please
I've become the rock upon the floor
The stone which broke the windows soul

Cast by the one I love
A stone does not feel
A stone does not cry
A stone never says goodbye

Broken glass, shards of glass
Picking up the pieces
For your children
My grandchildren
There's a reason they call me mom

Tomorrow I will hold them
And kiss them
As they violently cry
Having to tell them
You said goodbye

I will show them your note
And read what you wrote
I am picking up the pieces
with a broken heart

Walking upon broken glass
Not for you
Not for myself
But for these children
You left behind

For them, I bleed
For them, I sing

Farm land

The farmers became bankers
as the people ate grass

men and women ran like cattle
through the circus and hoops
lined in the metal chutes
branded with a numbered series
they rolled up their sleeves
for mercury
and formaldehyde
a d d

Everyone was fat
but so many were starving
like pigs, they got used to the shit
so they brushed their teeth every day
removing their instincts all the way
as they swallowed the lies of fluoride
aspartame was the cold stare
that tamed the wild beast

The farmers used the hands of Tesla
and played a monster's haarp
controlling everything
including the weather

The tv held their attention
and like a movie
Alfred Hitchcock played on cue
as they converted the corn into fuel

The stock market was rising
as the dollar was falling

the herd began selling their gold
and jewelry
along with their pride
and dignity
the joker misplaced sympathy's card
the donkey's eyes grew hard
then dull
the elephant raised its trunk
then fell

and the only thing that resembled liberty
was made by the mason's copper hand

The horses began to protest
and they all took a vote
then expected the farmer
to count them all up

in the newspaper clippings
written in black and white
the animals from the Middle East
became our enemy
none of the animals knew why
why every neighbor was an enemy
and some of the herd began questioning
why

the all seeing eye sat upon the pyramid
casting an eerie grin
but the camels had grown weary of the cracking whip
their postcards were sent
but the farmers had scrambled the scent

While the animals starved
and the barns rusted

the farmers prepared for war
snatching every chickens egg
The rooster cried out
but the coup flew to dallas
that's when the barbed wire went up

upon the backs of sweat and toil
the farmers read their fortune
they put cameras into every stall
of course, the sheep
didn't mind at all

and while war and chaos roamed the prairie
and satellites watched over the fields
a pack of wild dogs had remained hidden
carrying their own flag and message
a howl that groans in every creature

Their cries for freedom
sang to the full moon
but everybody knew
it wouldn't be long
before hunting season resumed

peasants and kings

blinded
we searched for the truth
for the open door
behind realities veil
a gateway through deja vu
a wall that peasants could not pass
for the king's castle is electronic
and the joker knows he'll die
if he reveals the secret
so he makes everyone laugh in riddles
while the sorcerer
creates a magic rhyme
called the american dream
like the pied piper they followed it
over the rivers of common sense
they built bridges to pass over it
wisdom cried through the third eye
as fluoride turned her heart to stone
so she cried to the sun
to shed some light
upon humankind
the digital walls were coming down
as the peasants found their own crown
so the kings of the world
turned the volume to chaotic
hoping the peasants would panic
but the poor were beginning to see
people like you and me
the illusion entity

The truth came in the light
shadows

there's no place like home

the wizard of oz spread the poppy like fruit
roasting the minds in a microwave of lies
cell phone suicide
poisoning the apples off to the side
the yellow brick road
was paved with the Georgia guidestones

the man behind the curtain
of red white and blue
began to speak with the voice of an octopus

"We gave the keys to Oliver Stone
then waited for the riots to unfold
seems the fluoride worked after all

pay no attention while we rape your children
behind the disguise of good intentions
brand you
with an SS number
you're going to need it
memorize it
unable to buy or sell
without
it

we'll convince you to vote
and that you are free
but you'll never guess the puppet master
pulling these strings

Get in line and don't say a thing
especially when boarding an airplane
give the pilots guns

while disarming the citizens
strip search
looking for bombs in breast milk
while weapons of mass destruction
blacken the gulf of Mexico
and Indian soil

the american people
the other white meat
it's what's for dinner
it's the american way
sex drugs and rock and roll
another dead soul
flushed down the toilet bowl

we'll spray your food with pesticides
inject your steak with steroids
color your food with herbicides
pollute the rivers and sea
until every fish contains mercury
you'll wash your hair with toxins
then paint your lips with aborted babies
while you protest outside the clinics

we'll build prisons
and call them schools
but the students cannot play
in the recesses of their own brain
handing them scripts of prozac nasal drips
we sheer the sheep
until they learn to fetch
follow the sticks
thrown here
there
everywhere
patriot act

clean water act
it's all an act
it's all a spin
a witch's brew

our plan began long ago
you never knew
that the bottle you fed your little baby
was coated with plastic venom
cribs lined with cross contamination
toys of lead paint
tainted milk

ignorance is strength
freedom is slavery
peace is war
You'll forget about 1984
big brother doesn't exist anymore
I'm just an mtv movie award

the land of the free..
the land of those too blind to see
it was us
who killed the dream"

and then I awoke...
and went back to sleep

there's no place like home

Independence

Traveled to this land for a chance of freedom
to make a place of our own

We escaped the inquisition
fleeing the killing spree of bloody England
We survived hardships and oceans
droughts and storms
Built our own houses with bare calloused hands
Planted our own vineyards with blood, sweat
and tears from burying so many friends across the journey's
way
I visit my daughter's grave
every single day

But today
the British are coming
Today we will stand
hand in hand
raising our battle flag

Brother standing with brother
ready to fight our
red coated brothers
The civil war everyone feared
is suddenly upon us here
Man the battle stations
Hide the women and children
load your muskets
and trim the oil lamps
for these nights
will be lit
by the fire in our eyes

The sounds of their British marching
rattles the fertile ground
Precision steps of fear
hauling their cannons nearer

A crescent moon dawns the night
The sky flashes bright
turning ghostly white
Booming explosions
Fire everywhere
Smoke and brimstone
filling the violenced air

Blood soaking the ground
under the thickened sound
of screaming widows and weeping orphaned children
Bullets fly upon the devil's canvas
This war plays out
with stars painted crimson red
Limbs flying in the shadows
Brothers dying
Shattered windows
Fractured bones
Burning homes

Surrounded by battalions
They've taken the bridge
and trapped our supply routes
Everyone wondering
who was the Judas among us

Betrayed by our own brother
into the hands of another
But retreat is not an option
Surrender is foreign upon our lips

Time for a new plan
Withdrawing closer
we'll take the battle to them
Every man for himself now
no turning back
With no armor to protect us
we shout our final battle cry

"Let each of
take one redcoat with us
before we perish"

We will die as free men
With freedom bleeding upon this new found land
Our Lexington homes
Our final tombstones

Yes
We will fight

We will bleed

We will die
But free
is where we will always be
Here

Ride Revere
Ride!

a king's awakening

heard the voice of a bird clear as day
singing a song of a wayward son
I wanted to stay
and age gracefully
but it nudged me along
said we have much work to do
jumped on my shoulder and hovered near my cheek
took a peek into my mouth
then whispered a little laugh

"I know where your heart is...
and I'm building a little nest
a place for faith and hope to rest
filled with peace
and all your favorite colors
take the kite out of your pocket
and come fly with me
come see
come see
'tis a garden of beauty
and land to behold
absent from cold in stunning glory
it's time
to proclaim yourself king
once more again

you stepped off the throne, for what you thought was a little
bit... ended up getting lost and losing your fingerprints
the crown you cannot see is still upon your head
just as it should be
all the mirrors have been distorted
your own twisted imagery
the scepter of power is firmly in your grip

but you let it slip
further and further away

Your Queen is awaiting you, my King
shall I lead the way?

won't you come fly with me?
won't you please
fly away..."

Are you the one?

Will you be my breath
when I can no longer breathe
Is it your voice I hear upon the slightest of breeze
a song I hear whisper through the trees

Are you the one?

The fire in your eyes reflecting off the mirrors in mine
becoming a trillion sunsets in the sky
Whose love becomes my sun
our souls woven together as one

Are you the one?

Whose lips have become my addiction
Your kiss, my only fix
To let me be wild, promising never to tame
our passion grows a red flame

Are you the one?

Whose body blankets me in cotton
who picks me up, when I have fallen
Lights my eyes, when they are darkened
returns the love that is given
That not only hears, but listens
who trusts me completely
never to question

Are you the one?

Would I be lost without you
Dead without you

The one whom I could tell everything and never feel ashamed
Will my last breath,
be Your name

Are my goals to lofty
set the bar too high
Can a King settle for anything less than a Queen

The Queen of my heart
I will give you the key to my kingdom
My heart is yours

Is there someone out there
does she really exist
Or should I pour all my dreams
upon the palm of my hand
And blow a farewell kiss

Just a corner

Sorry my love
For this misunderstanding
Never meant to smother you
and I don't want all of you
Just a piece of you, only a small part of you
Can you spare a corner of your heart?
just for me
This one small puzzle piece
placed inside of me
It's enough to keep me warm
my umbrella from the storm
That's all I need
Just a small piece of you
Like a small band-aid
To stop this bleeding
Just a drop to quench my thirst
Only a whisper
is all I need to hear
Softly in my ear
Just a corner of you
Can you spare that
for me
I understand if you can't
Can I hold your hand
one last time
Placed against my heart
Can I smell your scent
against your neck
Before you depart
please, take my note

You were the only button
that matched the sleeve of my heart

betting the farm

say it's forever
ever
say that we'll grow old
together
let our hearts become the feather
in the nest of trust
we'll feed the songs a wedding band

when I dream of you
I'm never me
just so much more

I saw our minds running
for the finish line
and our memories were the legs
the first day of school came
and I was so nervous
that first kiss
we studied grammar behind our chalkboard sheets
learning to read each other
with a light that played tag with tears of rain
the murmur of passion kissed our lips
touched the deep places between our hips
our embrace shrouded the world's scream
under the covers
we hid inside each others eyes
where words caressed our vocal chambers hair
and the breath of dreams
became a lover's dew

but those three words, couldn't cross the bridge
our eyes spoke love
but our mouths were frozen

four letters stuttering
we were both standing on the ledge
pondering the depths of the ocean
the rocks of past mistakes lined the shore below

staring into your soul
hold my hand
and we'll jump together
say it's forever
ever
that it's never going to end
say that we'll grow old together
and let this winter spring into summer
I'm jumping in
hope to see you at the bottom
saying
It's forever

1, 2, 3

I

l
o
v
e

y
o
u

life became our baby
with wrinkled hands we rocked her to sleep
forever came too soon

Sleep walking

Black lashed drapes
Dripping over pinpointed eyes
The fog from your lips
As smoke signaling clouds
I breathe you in
Moving in
Brown diamonds now dilated
Your lips touch mine
The heat of my heart
Melting upon your love
We dance in flames encircled
The fire in your eyes, now candled
The wolves howl in sync
Acting on instinct
Upon the sounds of a love
Once believed extinct
Crashing Light
The Curtains are opened
And gone is the dream
Awakened
 I scream
The Curtains now close
After sudden interruption
Fading to candy land
The land of my woman
My ghostly love
Who visits only through the night
When the world becomes quiet
The sun blackened by twilight

Back to Black lashed drapes
Hanging over pupils eclipsed
The mist from your lips

Becomes our shroud
Hidden from the world
Nightmares not allowed

Only in my sleep
Do you fly to me
Only in my sleep
Do you see me
Only in my sleep
My sleep
My love
My black dove
My ghostly love
Only in my sleep

you took my breath away

risen from the dead
from your elven cast spell
you took all my ashes
and made so many wishes
they all came true
I opened up my eyes
cold and empty
you stoked the fire
massaged my heart
gave me CPR
brought me back from death
your essence
your aura
your being
sonar waves of truth and honesty
you were the key
removing these shackled hands
melted feet of quicksand
you held your breath
and went down to the depths
fought the demons of hell
claiming your king
from the land of the dead
shaking your friend awake
sleeping all wrong
nightmares all long
spoken into sleepwalking ears
followed me into traffic
stopped all the cars
led me back home
into you
you waited out the coma
offering your own blood

praying to the God of your fathers
to give sight to this blind man
your man
I am yours
you wrapped me in blankets
bringing color back to flesh
taught me how to walk again
taught me how to laugh again
taught me how to live again
my teacher
my love
my bride
I am yours
you gave me life
for without love
everything is dead
a crippled man runs again
a leper is healed
you broke this cave man
out of iced shield
took my snowball shaped heart
wrapped it in your hands
your arms
wrapped inside my lighthouse
my lifeguard
my everything
my all
my life
my love
breathing your breath
your lips pushing into my soul
you're all I can feel
your scent
savoring this sip of wine
afraid I'm flying to high
for all I see are clouds

you and me
floating upon nothing
blue eyes of soft steel
my hand a magnet
to your skin
hair
down your back
bringing you closer
daring to open eyes
to find you looking into mine
your eyes smile
then deep and hard
intense
your claws come out
claiming me as yours
taking the lead in this dance
both hands on tender cheeks
as your tips run down my back
becoming one
burning flesh
can't believe your mine
can't help myself
I love you
you brought me back to life
life becoming alive
growing
deeper
deeper
into Love

into Life

14 years ago

How do fourteen years disappear?
where did they go
we held onto the past
as long
as hard as we could
yet it passed us by
before we learned to fly
left us
standing still
caught between spring and winter
when neither of us
were looking ahead

and I wonder
if yesterday's memory has a home
does it have a soul
do the years ever get cold
cause every time I think of you
to the time we knew before
reality plays those familiar songs
when we both
were so wrong
and so right
the future seemed so bright

our hearts were fragile way back then
like the tears before the fall
we flew upon the wings of youth
until the world became a wall

and yesterday is all I can see sometimes
it's all I've ever known
they say that karma's a bitch

you reap what you have sown
but if only I had known
cause summer never looks the same
not the way it did before

summer never looks the same
without you by my side
wish I could build a time machine
and go back
to the time we knew before

cause my love never died for you
it's screaming in these words
the hands of strangers never feel the same
all I can feel is the wind and the rain
burning my skin until it's re(a)d
just like my beating heart bled

if only I known the end
from the beginning
we never would have parted
if only I knew then
what I know now
I wouldn't be singing this song
how do fourteen years disappear
where did they go
cause the summer never looks the same
not the way it did before
and summer never looks the same
not the way
it did
before

endangered in love

the place where endangered species willing sacrifice their
lives

dark chocolate eyes,
imported from France
a pair of deliciousness boxed in soft velvet flesh
soft hill of butterfly wing
singing through two rivers
two caves which echo
moans of tender delight

Queen and King of our mouthly kingdom
two heated bakeries becoming one fire
your saliva lotioned in lavender and chamomile
where tongues rule the moment
smearing, feeling, slowing,
sword playing, dancing
laughing, eloping
silence all around us locked in this embrace
Shrouded in enchanted ecstasy
a halo of love envelops us
lifting us
taking us
to infinities eternal dreams

lips of natural sugar
taste of wine
red licorice tongues entwined

hummingbird heartbeat
fingers in slow motion
gently tracing your outline
reading your skin

with blind fingers
taking it all in
breathing your scented trail
fields of poppies play lullaby sleep
Liberation hearts
with Tinkerbell trust

American
Switzerland
Brazilian
African
Different souls
shades of skin
different voices
all the same to me
the most beautiful creatures
God has ever made

the matador's cape

Inhibitions
lying naked
on the bedroom floor
Passion lit
incense
filling closed door
Through stained glass bedroom windows

You let your hair down long
Locks of raven flowing with grace
Shuts out the world
Staring now, face to face
Your breath, the only wind I seek
Your heart, I hear it speak
Loudly pounding upon my chest, my little earthquake
This trembling I cannot escape

Looking deeper into brown eyed honesty
Into the future I see
Forming one ocean with thee
Your loving gaze directly into mine
Softer than your ivory laden skin
Deeper and deeper
They draw me in
Like magnets to metal
Me the match, You the candle

Your passionate breath
As a fiery river flowing down my neck
Slow motioned down further down
I now taste your vanilla warm lips

Exploring the volcano
Your mouth as sizzling lava

Dancing tongues of fire
Amidst molten hot saliva

A tiny bead of saltwater
Lightly trickles from your shimmering skin
Dripping onto seldom opened mouths and entering within

Your taste
Your scent
A lure I can't escape
Your blood red lips
The matador's cape

My eyes like an artist's hand
Gently tracing your face
Two of the most beautiful flowers ever born
A pair of dark golden Irises
Encompassing the black full moon
I find myself lost in the eyes of angels
Eclipsed by mascara painted petals

Slowly you rise now, effortlessly
Hovering in mid air
A fraction away from skin bare
A string from our own woven silk
Stretching from our last kiss

My princess
My love
My forever black dove
Your smile, now shining upon me
Is as black light fluorescence
Lighting this tiny space in between us
A cherubim aura around your face
Freedom found
in your loving embrace

Look into My soul now
And hear these unspoken words
These crevices under my eyes
Are but canyons caused from rivers run dry
This beard was my forest
From which I could hide
Didn't think you would notice me
Even if you tried
This unkept stringy long hair
Blankets my face as a jungle of vines
But you saw the star
And followed all the signs

Through my walls and barbed wire fences you hacked through
Whispering, "Dear Prince, my enchanted forest is you'"
My fairy tale ending, finally come true

Dear Diary... I've been having the same visions now, over and over for the past week
Not quite knowing what it all means, but it leaves me so weak

Not sure how long I can hold onto this dream
That's why I write them all down, upon your pages of cream

Guess I'm hoping these writings are somehow prophetic
Stranger's eyes speaking 'just how pathetic'

Fun to pretend that I'm like John of Revelation
But fearing all along, it's only my imagination

Maybe like Harry Potter, this pen is my magical wand
Touching these pages, transforming them into my Swan

Better yet
This inkhorn, the stone, and my pen is Excalibur

I'll slay the dragon's heart, rescue my Queen and marry her
Take her to my castle
Surrounded by moats of silken flow
To the chamber of stained-glass window
Where French braided rope of raven's wing
Hang gently down as a waveless stream
I'll climb up this life-line
To where my sunshine
Becomes my soul's wine

But Dear Diary...
Please just keep it a secret, if by some chance you already
know
That this pencil I hold
Is only a cigarette in my hand
Leaving only flicks of ashes
In the bitter end.

Once again

We found ourselves

then we found each other

born from the same cloud
we became snowflakes together
swirling and dancing
laughing and chasing

the Creator's breath
blew us past the chapters of religion and philosophy
we skipped upon the second hands
we skipped stones with Father Time
we skipped past kindergarten and first grade
we opened our eyes and received our diploma
took three deep breaths
taking photos in between
noticing all the mirrors had vanished
along with our pride and innuendo
the only thing I could see
was you
you
placing your hands upon my hips
gently drawing me in
and we became one

your lips were questioning
but your eyes
your eyes were already at the finish line
dilated wide
with specks of silver green petals
the sun was rising in between them
you uttered a chord causing our passion to grow

the warmth began blowing over the sleeves of my heart
your mind guided me through the misty dark
and we swayed through the blossoms of cherry trees
the moans of frenzy
ecstasy
like a kite
commanding the breeze
we held onto the rope
until our hands were red

our love
grew into the raging fires that painted the desert sand with
watercolor
and the shadow of our faith
was tinted in every shade of golden hue
we made our own beds from freshly picked linens
slept upon our own oasis
and all our nightmares became hallucinations

we gathered our illusions like firewood
kindled them with every possible delusion
stuffed them all upon a sinking boat
whispered, "God bless you"
then lit a match and cast it upon the sail
left it burning in the oceans of our past

and suddenly the rays of the sun shone brighter than ever
before
and all our secrets
kept hidden under beds
and puffed up eye lids
bled
then ran
all the monsters fled
their costumes came off
and all the prisoners

were finally forgiven and let go
the remnants of our embrace
kept all the gardens watered and warm

we danced beside the fragments of our insecurities
made love upon the scales of justice
etched our names into marble monuments
unclenched fists with painted fingertips
Our hearts were pure as virgin eyes
blind to the world around us
we were free
free

the forest was our home
our feet
became soft and tender
there was no gravel
no sharp stones or city lights
no screams scratching through the eerie nights
only the whispers from Cupid's arrow
like a soft pillow
blankets us good night
we ate from the lips of gods
our wings were long
our will was strong
we took all our memories
and promises unfulfilled
tied them in yellow ribbons
and flew like angels around the world

the acid rain from the worlds polluted mouth
spat at our backs, but we refused to taste it
surrounded by riddles
we held our ground
the oceans tempest
threatened to destroy us

we found safety in each other's arms

we held onto Truth
tossed the anchor of Love
sang songs with Hope and Faith
then flew our hands up high
and laughed at the rising tide

we swallowed the Good Book
and spit out all the seeds
closed the doors behind us
and fell to our knees
cried out for Wisdom
then met Her at the gates
She became our tutor
She became our friend

learning from all of our past mistakes
we scribbled our sins upon paper airplanes
then set them on fire before they could fly again

we silently watched them burn
then took all the ashes
along with some blood that had spilled
fed them to the wind
and her anger was quelled
and soon
everything became quiet
our hearts
full of peace
wisdom again
began to speak
one last time
but she never said goodbye
she only smiled and winked
as we had learned to read between the lines

two hearts
are stronger than one

we hugged knowledge
and kissed understanding a hundred times
just before they gave us two cans of graffiti
told us to spray paint the world
we followed their fingers
to the signs of the times
and all the commercials
for the "End of the World"
we painted a big circle through them
and a thick line in between
sometimes a big yellow U turn
would make us both smile
and with our last pennies
we bought a calendar
circled the date
Doomsday
just to remind the world
the prophecy
was wrong again
and everyone who had lived in fear
and put their lives on hold
began to celebrate
and live
once again

Cicerone ~ a guide, especially one who takes tourists to
museums, monuments, or architectural sites and explains
what is being seen

You hide them
Disguise them
Vanish cream them away
You see ugliness
but to me, you're flawless

These lines
Like a 9 month diary tattooed
Every line an emotion
They take me down memories lane

Remembering all those crazy food cravings
you desired at the time
Still sound funny to me
Vlasic pickles and Breyers ice cream

Propped up in bed with the lights down low
reading every possible name slow
Like a pregnant gunslinger
shooting down all my recommendations
Although I still like Thor and Ariel
the others I can't recall
Finally said, you're the one going through all the pain
you can pick the baby's name

Your stomach growing larger by the day
Eating for two, in line at the buffet
Just getting up became a struggle and a fight
Massaging your legs and feet every night

The cold gel and the ultrasound
Thought it was a boy
but couldn't tell for sure
Suddenly it all became real
Especially when I could feel
the baby kick for the very first time
Always in the back of my mind

Walking through all the store aisles
hand in hand, upon our own little isle
Trying to determine which crib and stroller were the best

Plugging every outlet
Child proofing the rest

Three in the morning
And suddenly the weather changed
The most violent of storms ripping through your body
Your white knuckled grip upon the hospital bed
I tried to hold you down
But you were like a raft upon a hurricane sea
Telling you everything was going to be okay
But knowing you couldn't hear me
The lightning and thunder
became your contractions and screams
Seemed to last throughout the night
But morning came
soon giving way to a peaceful rain
The sun suddenly emerging
Holding our baby together
We basked in the light
You said she looked like me
I said the same, back to you

So when you awake in the middle of the night
And find my head gently resting upon your chest
My fingers sweetly tracing your belly
Please do not brush my hand aside
Just having a hard time sleeping
Sometimes I just don't want to talk about it
And even though I don't show it
Occasionally I feel a little bit weak
And these lines remind me of your strength
Without words, they speak
Telling me
that in the end
We are going to be okay

You don't like them I know
but to me, they are like the left over petals
from the rose you gave birth to
If you could only see them through my eyes
and the love I have for you
Then maybe, you'd be okay with them too

the morning of winter's water

it rose above the lunar shadow
with soft tones of red layers
I fell in love with you there

heaven's umbrella sparkled perfume
scents of clover and lilac
whispered secrets upon the Northern winds
with a smile riding on the dandelion wishes
the sun hid its flame
for it was ashamed of the love that coursed through our veins

everything so beautiful
rested upon your every breath
and your heartbeat
played my song
with your arms of pearl draped around my neck
our honesty became our fortress
we planted a garden of faithfulness
their flowers became the cross we bore
and the nectar of frankincense
gold and myrrh
filled our minds with dreams never dreamt before

we took the last green maple leaf
and wrapped its promise around our fingertips
holding each other's soul
we knew this gold could never be broken

I held your wing
and you held mine
and one angel
we did become

terminal

I hid my secrets in the ashes of yesterday's news
buried my regrets under the sheets of tomorrow
erased the smiles off my dreams and drew them laughing
pooled all my tears and swam
sang songs that made the mockingbird jealous

learning to sing
learning to swim
learning to see

the tooth fairy came to me
said it heard the reaper whispering
said it wanted to warn me
only one year left
before death
would take me

the news took me to my knees
prayed for God to give me the strength
to forgive all my enemies
asked Him
to teach me to fly
on these borrowed wings of mine

learning to be
learning to die
learning to fly

I counted those I loved
then took a piece of my heart
and gave it to everyone
said, "I'm going to miss you
All of you

but I've got some things to do."
promised I'd be back within a year
and that's when I met you

you took my scars
and washed away the pain
I always kissed you
in the pouring rain

but time was flying
and soon
I'd be dying
so I gazed into your eyes
for as long as I could
for when I did
time stood still

learning to breathe
learning to love
learning to cherish the time we have

how do I tell you now?
will you think I've deceived you?

I'll pretend tomorrow
is just another day
make you breakfast
just the way
I do every day

couldn't sleep that night
tossing in bed
the nightmare screaming
inside my head

walked to the park that morning
and neither of us
saw that truck
coming

without thinking
I pushed you to safety
then landed twenty feet
further away

the tears fell from your cry
you fell to your knees
screaming
"You can't leave me
please God
don't let him go

No...

No...

please

just hold on baby
please

don't go

Oh God... Somebody help us!

I never knew how I would die
but with you by my side
I lived more in one year
than most do
in a lifetime

and if I had known the end
from the beginning
I want you to know
I'd do it
all over again

you bit your vanilla glossed lips
then disappeared
behind the eclipse

requests

the wind plays my favorite song
skipping tracks - the sins of my past
listening to my soundtrack
I pause and play it again
upon an island in a sea of memory
where I felt I belonged
thought would last
thinking about you
thinking about me
thinking about us
and how we used to be

the sun is shining mirror's red
but here I am
lying in bed
for that's where you remain
out of my heart
but still in my head
so I sleep
for in my dreams
the memories top the ice cream
and I melt in your eyes
your lips wet
and your scent of sweet kisses
my forever sunset of coconut cream

the sun is still rising
but the angels don't nest here anymore
empty and cracked
crimson turned hollow
can't think about tomorrow
it's yesterday which I travel
but the forks in the road are all

broken gravel
thinking about you
thinking about me
thinking about us
and how we used to be
rusty locks and broken keys
all wrapped in this fortune cookie

caught your flash in a photograph
the years have treated you kind
but time
time never comes with rainbows
only shadows
maybe it never was
I know it will never be
just thinking about you and me
just thinking here
going to sleep
and that's where we'll meet
holding love
between our breath

sweet dreams

sweet dreams

She said she was tired
said she needed to lie down
and get some rest
she just wanted to sleep
she needed some peace
and quiet
if only for a moment

She walked to the bathroom
with a slight pause in her step
returning with a stumble in her step
walking back a little more limp
diazepam lips
in a halo of nicotine sticks

She hugged me hard and long
I said, "Is something wrong?"

"No baby...
I'm just tired
just need to lie down
and go to sleep
can you turn down the music please."
then her shadow disappeared
under the silken sheets

Fast forward

911
'Oh God nooooooooo'

Sir... what is your emergency

"Jessie! Jessie! Wake up!"
Crying
"She's not moving!"
Screaming
"oh God help us'"

Sir calm down and explain what is happening

"My girlfriend... she she she...

Sir?

"She's not breathing!'

We need to start CPR... I can walk you through this...

"She's cold
She's so cold...
oh God nooo
no
I think she's dead
I think she's dead

I
think

she's
dead

Time stands still
said she needed to lie down

and go to sleep
she wanted to rest
she said she needed peace and quiet
if only for a moment
and all I could do
was say
Sweet Dreams

Sweet Dreams
not
'I love you'
I didn't even kiss her
so now I sit here
with a gun to my head
wondering if I should call 911
or end it all
not sure which trigger to pull
Sweet Dreams
that's what I said
and I can't forgive myself for that

nobody
forgives me
I have no tears left

Time stands still
there is no going forward
she said she was tired
that's all I can see
just need some rest
and peace
if only for a moment
I beg for sleep
as my shadow disappears
under these silken sheets

only the frames remain

She's dead now
and I can't see her anymore

I close my eyes tight
but everything is blank
it's all black

I search for a memory
deep inside
but they allude me
I want to find them
hold them
kiss them
live them
but they are hiding
and I don't know
if I'll ever find them
again

so all I do is stare

I stare at her pictures
still hanging on the walls
but all these photographs are empty
they don't speak
they don't say a thing
but still I stare
wanting them to sing

there is a dead space inside of me
where she is supposed to be
I've done my soul searching

and came up empty
there is nothing left of her
but there should be
something
anything
but there is nothing
except an empty hole inside of me

all I want is a memory
I've cried
I've prayed
I'm cursed to live the rest of my days
without her
and all I am left with
is a wondering
wondering why
everyone else can remember
but I

She's dead now

seems the pain was too much to bear
and now everything my eyes saw and ears heard
have been erased
everything she did
erased
never again to see the light of day
never again
to be heard from
or seen
her touch
just a dream

and all I can do now
is stare into nothing

I didn't kill her
but I buried her
and now she's gone
and all I am left with
is nothing
except
a wanting

somewhere
behind these brown eyes
is a blue coldness
a frozen numbness
behind this laugh
is a silent sigh
a missing step
a missing beat
a missing memory
of you and me

and so I take the memories from others
and paint my own colors
but it's all convoluted
it's not real
because without a memory
I can't even dream of you

so I'll close my eyes tightly
once again
and tonight
the tears will roll down
once again
and I'll try and search for you
as my lips beg to scream
how could I have forgotten you

she's dead now
even in my dreams
I can't bring her back to life
and that
is the empty memory that haunts me in my waking dreams

Time's windowsill

it was death at a funeral
in late December
that brought me back to you
your ghostly shadow
caressed the petals I left

broken violin strings
played atop your grave
the wind picked them up
and played them against my cheek like wind chimes
roses bloomed as I held your hair
kissing the air
I waited there
until my spirit disappeared

walking to the car
I made a wish upon a star only I could see
in my dreams

I unlocked the door
to an empty house
and felt the metal
click
fall to the floor

silence
in the shattered darkness
the paralysis grew cold as alarm bells ran
time was moving
away from me

my mind quivering
eyes spinning
the pen in my hand became a broken limb
refusing to sway in the wind
the air began to bleed
as my hand could not write
what the heart cannot see

lost
in a photograph
icicles dripped the darkest of ink
the rain dropped keys
black ivory upon my skin
your voice grew heavy
your scent cloudy
then the storms finality
as your memory
became my tomb

glossy eyes

the cigarette drips
my thoughts fall with the ashes
these memories of mine
suffer insomnia
rewind
pause
then back again

the static screams
'Don't waste your time'
the songs come and go
the fog rolls in
the wind begins to chime

the courage
hides under the ashes
the flames of yesterday
blew away with your ghost

foolish games

This crevice in my chest
This crater you left behind
This shattered heart
that you tore apart
Only left with blackness
Fallen into this cave
Hanging by a thread
Holding onto leftover dreams
Making wishes
with violent screams
No one can hear me
it seems
Swinging and dropping
further into this darkness
The light of hope
nowhere to be found
Tears dripping upon the floor
each tear a plea for you
to return
But they only splatter, my love
against an empty wall
Only echo inside myself
Seems there's no one here
A walking
Talking
Empty
Shell
Wanting to let go
and fall into this abyss
The taste of your lips
the love upon your kiss
It's what keeps me holding on

Heard others say to follow your heart
never thought it would lead me here
A haunting ghostly fear
So hollow
So cold
So alone
Never knew how much you meant to me
Trapped
A prisoner, once free
As two love birds we flew
into the sky past the sun
around heaven's eye
We were the whisper
upon Cupid's lips
The secret shadow
behind the lunar eclipse
Memories like tombstones now
dusty and vanishing away
Took my breath away
Took my spirit away
Just withering away
My soul, a consuming black hole
You were the star of my galaxy
The warmth of my world
Still hanging on
Blindly
Hoping
Fading
Down
My strength frayed
Feel I'm drifting away
Never knew one could die
in the blink of an eye
From a love
that has died
Your foolish games

my Russian roulette
No guns or drugs needed
it was you
walking away
that did it
A love once real
now a corpse
like me
Seeing a great light
like so many have said
Angelic voices telling me to come
But I want to stay
just one more day
with you
In your arms
in your eyes
in your heart
than eternity away

Now

If I run to your arms, will you hold me?
If I ran to your heart, would you forgive me?
If I cried tonight, would you hurt me?
If I died tonight, would you cry for me?

Would you hold me as I fall down?
Or will you let me go
and watch me drown?
Will you carry me?
could you carry me?
Will you hold me in your arms?
Not forever... not forever
Only right now... only right now

Because today is my birthday and it feels like my funeral
I feel like I'm dead and only your love can make me alive
again
Today is my birthday... but it feels like my funeral
I'm choking and drowning and I can't breathe
I'm hoping you can make me alive again
Only you, only right now

If I gave you my heart, would you take it?
would you bury it?
I'm giving you my heart
will you take it?
will you let it fall?
Please tell me now... only right now...
I only need your love right now...
Not yesterday or tomorrow
only today, only right now

Because today is my birthday, and it feels like my funeral
I feel like I'm dead, and only your love can make me alive
again
Today is my birthday… but it feels like my funeral
I'm choking and drowning and I can't breathe,
I'm hoping you can make me alive again
Only you, only right now
Only you
Right now
Now

crematory ashes in November's wind

every time
I see the leaves falling
like today
I think of you
in autumns colors I remember my heart bleed
cinnamon eyes
brown sugared lips
I couldn't save you from yourself
and over time
every time
I see the moon
I remember your eyes eclipsed
slowly slamming shut
the stars fell that night
erasing the zodiak
and the universe
my world was in chaos
there was nowhere to hide
and all I could do was watch
as Leo attacked Virgo
and the Scorpion chased after her children
an implosion
a supernova
a heart's explosion
a blackhole
sucking the light out of thunder's roll
there was no escaping
the agony from your silence
You had gone
but you left everything unborn
undone
haunting

alone

every time
I feel the cold
I think of you
and how you
just drifted away...

I don't know where you went to
but God knows I tried to follow
now
everything
is so hollow and empty and meaningless and seemingly
endless...

The colors are turning blood red
the trees are bleeding
the sky is anemic
heavily breathing
nature's warning
that winter is coming
every time
I try to forget you

I wonder
do you remember me
do you think of me
or have you erased me
destroyed me
buried me

every time the leaves begin to fall
I remember the trickle of blood
running down my back
from the knife
engraved with your prints

and I think back
to a time before
when we seemed to complete each other
sentences
weren't needed
to a time before
when our smiles were full of joy
and sticky like cotton candy
we painted our rooms yellow
and danced with the canaries
you were young and I was stupid
we took the ceiling off the bedroom
and the feeling
that you wished never went away
just turned to dust
and disappeared

every time
I think of the time before
I only want you more

Our love was the ghost of the seasons
never thought that our spring and summer
would end in a pile of colorless leaves
dry and crumbling
just lying still
forever more
the kind of dead leaves
that children don't want to play in
anymore

and even so...

I wish you were here

just one more wish

to touch you one last time
to properly say goodbye
with a long hard embrace
imprinting your scent into a memory bank
to look into your eyes one more time
we wouldn't have to say anything
I believe our tears would say it all
and if we had a chance
I don't think either one would walk away
again
but it's just a dream
and life is too short
to waste upon dreaming...
It's time to make new dreams come true
but I will miss you
and every time the leaves fall
I will say thank you
and a prayer
for you
my love
my forever black dove

fly away
be free

apocalypse now

One red rose

Sleeping atop a bed of coffin

Everything we had

Died with you

This is the end

Your journey now beginning

Mine sealed shut
With pall bearers grip

You've left me here
All alone

I like to think you can hear me
Sitting here in front of your tombstone
Just wish my name was next to yours
Carved and engraved

I'm so dead
But they say
I'm lucky to be alive

You were my luck
My dream
Wishbone
Fantasy

The skies are cloudy and dark
It's starting to sprinkle
Watering these flowers
With my tears

Wish I could stay here forever
Right by your side
I'm going home now
This castle so empty and lonely quiet

All those little things that got on my nerves
I just adore them now
Wish I could have told you that

Haven't washed your clothes yet
They still have your scent

It's hard walking away from you
Always was
Still is
Even now
My last image of you
In your flowing black gown

Still have your voice on the answering machine
I can't erase it

People say I've got to move on
But you were everything to me
And now you're gone

My only dream buried now
Your beginning
became
my end

Half past 10

It was love at first sight...

we flew higher than the kites
too soon
but neither of us
were ready for the winds of change that blew

the rainbows suddenly grew lightning bolts
and the robins
dropped dead
serving you breakfast in bed
I remember looking at the time

your hunger chopped off my head
but it was your tongue
that pierced my heart
I had just finished building the wall
when you knocked on the door
said please
can I come in

I welcomed you into my fortress
showed you everything
inside the closet

You covered my eyes
singing hush
don't cry
I'm going to make everything
alright

The song of angels
placed me on cloud nine
I just didn't see the demons
behind
those eyes

I still remember
I won't let myself forget
it's in my skin
this sin
buried deep within
she said, "I don't love you anymore"
that's when her voice changed
and I couldn't understand another word

I watched her eyes change color
her lips grew into foreign soil
the tension
grew a knot
a rope that could never be climbed

it all became a silent movie
and the black and white never became more clearer
all the pain...
that came

and came again
I engraved them into wooden blocks
built a bridge
and burned them
this heart... still beating
has already began building
another wall

the memories?
amazing how the mind can hide things from the soul

I've paid the toll
paid the artist
to paint those final words
into my wrist
like a watch...
an automatic timer

it reminds me of that silent movie
the one that keeps playing inside my head
but at the same time
it reminds me
how we once held hands
reminds me
of once upon a times
when you still loved me
before your words
forever burned me

So I tell myself
my anthem
my mantra
I don't love you anymore
I don't love you anymore
I love you
more

but it never comes out right
look at the time
time to try again...
but all I hear
all I can say
are her words
every day
echoing inside my head
"I don't love you
anymore"

that's all I hear anymore
and I can't bear it
anymore
I don't want to hear it
anymore
but here it comes again
half past ten
I don't love you
anymore

The Screenplay

Your eyes captured the essence of diamonds
but the memories of your heart
rusted
and when they swung in my mind
I cut myself
to remind myself
I still bleed red

You cried for the head of John the Baptist
said you were just playing a part
but somewhere behind the veil
I knew it was my heart
you would eventually eat
'would you like another piece?'

I fed your lips of grapes
with my soul in vinegar and wine
followed by a shot of disgrace
our faces
mingled with the rich and famous
the pictures they took
front page tabloids news
I never knew
you would strip yourself bare
trading dignity for anal applause

the flashes from the paparazzi pack
brought the actress out in you
and the worst in you
fighting to keep a smile upon your face
you devoured your own flesh
nocturnal
cannibal

I reached out my hands
soft and gentle
but
you thought I wanted something
that was the least of it
I never wanted anything from you
money is only paper

I wanted your heart
that was all
nothing more
I dreamt of sharing snowflakes and angels
but you couldn't open the walls
nailing them shut with the nails that crucified the Christ

Diamonds to Rust
you played the part
paranoid

two parts, half full

the phone call of a misplaced dial
made you push the rewind button
you fell back into the screams you thought you had left
and now I'm left
paying for the sins of every lover that betrayed your faith
the crimes of adultery left your mind altered
you forgot who I was
began calling me
by her name
until I was no longer beautiful
in your eyes

I thought you were the one
my queen of heaven
my skin was hard
but your eyes of toffee brown
they melted the mystique

lost for so long
your voice sang songs of home

called you my princess
under the sheets of scented candle
but you were the devil in disguise
I should have known otherwise

We built a house of trust
with pink ribbons and steel mesh
still suspicious
you never closed the nightmare's chapter

it was girls night only
and I thought you might be lonely

that's why I rented Lord of the Rings
your favorite movie
after 20 text messages
my friends
finally convinced me to just hang up
I thought you
I thought we
were stronger than that

My friend saw you at that bar
You said I couldn't come
now I know why
dressed in your black dress
Johnny said you were flirting
you should have said no
when Spanish lips asked you to dance
You could have refused the free drinks
but no
laughing and drinking and having a good time
you must think I've lost my mind
been down this road before
and I'm not afraid to show you the door

I don't know where it all went wrong

I would look into my crystal ball
but it's cracked
like my mind
my soul
my heart
it bleeds
it screams
I love you

but I don't know
what to do
I don't know anything
except how to drink
the pain only becomes numb
like a detached limb
I can still feel you
and in the recesses of my mind
I still want you

How could I ever forgive you?
How could I ever put my trust in you?
thought you were my soul mate
checkmate
scratch that
Dear Diary...
I'm in hell

I still carry your photo in my purse
don't know why
after you called me a whore
I shut the door
you wanted to know if I was crying
My god...
how pathetic are you

and yet
in the distance
I hear your voice
I wish we could tear some pages
and go back
to the beginning
when you called me Juliet
I wish we could do that

Can't sleep
asking myself
why does a broken heart love the darkness so much
I have some problems
only wish life had dealt me a better hand
I wish you could understand
when I give my heart
I give all of it
and now
there's not a shred of evidence
grown men aren't supposed to cry
and yet
I hear you singing in the distance
I wish we could tear some of these pages
and go back
to the beginning
when you called me Romeo
and start all over

Frayed

The bird's song fell
as the air stood still
and the color from Autumns leaves
died

she laid there
became a chameleon
blending in
with the bleeding

with his back against a tree
he tried to erase the memory
but the carvings were too deep
falling asleep
his heart lay naked
bare
cold
scared

they were both dying
becoming nothing
everything they believed
mocked them in the end

they were both hiding
in the corner of a shadow
they were both crying
and the streets never felt
so hollow

stones became their pillows
their only friend
the weeping willow

under sheets of poison ivy
they slept
the past had become a trap
and neither of them
could escape
the cremation
their tears became one river
from years turned bitter
but the dream they planted
so long ago
one day began to grow
choking on the sands of time
they both began walking
at the same time
and as they drank the memories they released
their lips met
the sun fell

an everlasting love
that was always meant to be
painted the clouds in dream
her fingers of piano keys
played his hair softly
he struck the chords so gently
she found trust again
and they both lived happily
ever after
the melody of their love
screamed with passion
and soon
the pain of the past
was freed at last
and the music they made
left them
unafraid

here I am

You took my breath away
Yet
Here I am
Still breathing
You were once my angel
But now
Here I am
My companion, the angel of death
You were my rainbow
Now
Here I am
Holding blood and ashes

You were the light at the end of my tunnel
But now
Here I am
Becoming nocturnal

You burned my hopes like garbage
Yet
Here I am
Still walking

You carried my dreams into oblivion
But still
Here I am
Dreaming of what could have been

You stole my heart
Yet
Here I am
Dead
I want my heart back

It's time

Holding on
to a fairy tale
all gone wrong
placed my soul into your hand
gave you my everything
faithfulness
rewarded
with emptiness
alone beside you
bleeding your name
in love with a pet rock
even given a nickname
the fire in your eyes
dimmed
to a cold flame
your touch no longer warm
bumps upon my skin
empty words
empty passion
this ring upon my finger
cold
as your eyes
steel
as the cage you placed me in
tight
as your control
only a string
tied
like my wings
golden reminder
that you aren't the one
Believe it's time
to find a new sky

hourglass tipped
our wedding day
the sands now empty
telling me
it's time
to hope again
to breathe again
to dream again
to fly again
to rise again
to laugh again
to live again
to be myself again
It's time
to stop holding on
to this fairy tale
all gone wrong
held on far too long
hands and palms
raw and cut
bleeding your name
It's time to let go
Time to heal
goodbye my dear

burnt wax with vanilla red

vanilla tipped roses
thorns around your lips
your rattle and hiss
remind me
this was never a memory of you
it was never meant to be
you
and I
flew too high
upon the wings of fallen angels
the abyss is now your home

barely living above ground
lying in your grave
it is this memory that saves me
from the thorns around your lips
when your scent blows a kiss
vanilla tipped roses
scars around my wrist
scabs around my heart
bleeding from a wound
deeper than your absent kiss
I will miss
the forgotten memories
wishing them
Goodbye

when summer brings vanilla tipped roses
walking into my broken windows
of memory
whispering in my ears
around my mouth

into my eyes
then into my life
only to die in my heart

leaving my vanilla tipped dreams
erasing themselves
alone
at the end of darkness
and your heart
just out of reach

Thank you sir, may I have another?

another hair turned gray today
the wrinkles of time
sketched into my forehead
another starless sky
another last goodbye
another black eye
another door shut
another push
another shove
another stumble
in my step
another riddle
left unkept
another puddle
dripping wet
another mystery
wrapped up tight
another long sigh
on this sleepless night
holding my rose-colored glasses
tight
tighter than I ever have
in my life
the silent steps of paranoia
creeping near
fragility lined with despair
another state of mind
is never far behind
another second wasted
another leaf
left unturned
another bridge burned
another year

buried
another present
returned to sender

the glasses are fine
it's when I close my eyes
I'm momentarily paralyzed

the ghosts of the past
hold onto my eyelids
closing them shut
wanting to live again
and torment me
for just a little bit
longer

Sad but true

Her life
flashed before her eyes
and that's the last thing
she ever saw

She never saw
that car coming
never heard
the train coming
the hand
coming

she saw everything escalating
began stepping
on eggshells
when he
was around
she saw the weather forecast
clear as day
but she never saw herself changing
pink ribbons for prison clothing

all of her dreams
were only memories
of the past

she couldn't see through the blur
the train was whistling
the brakes were screeching
but she could not foresee
this catastrophe

the car was coming
this train could not be stopped
the hand finally came
that's when she saw
that's when she screamed
but it came too late

now she can't see anything
the world is mute
left in a wheel chair
playing cards with fate

Take care

I thought I had risen
above temptation
but there it stood - hovering
reaching down with salivating hands
all the time
a cold wind blew
as it exhaled
slowly
blue and white bled into grey
causing all the little doves
to fly away
crushed eggs and broken sticks
fell
with my surprise
the cross on the wall
turned itself upside down

Walking through the snowstorm
I broke free from the sheets of ice
the umbrella broke down
but my feet were still warm

The tales of gold were told upon the trail
with my ear to the ground
I heard the Calvary's hoof beat

the flavors from mother earth
and her delicious scents
held me to her skin
but in order to live
I had to die
so I finally kissed her
and said goodbye

please wipe your feet, before stepping on me

the red came in your screams
red ants that formed a colony of pain
inside my brain
the agony could not escape

the blue grew with the colors of despair
in the empty embrace of broken promises
cracked beyond recognition
solitary dandelion wishes
your lies sliced my wrist
until my faith became anemic
every flower I held wilted

inside the spinning of my thoughts
you traced my love with ashes of indigo
leaving a frozen trail
a once upon a time beating heart
now
so cold and hollow
the hurricane comes in the silence
that's when I hide inside the echo

the yellow replaced the streaks of courage
I once carried upon my back
putting a pause in my step
and a burden upon my shoulders

I couldn't even carry myself
the last remnants of dignity
I gathered like crumbs
came begging on hands and knees
the crack of your smile
broke my spine

but it was the blade in your tongue
that pulled the life support

your eyes of hazel green
walked inside the prowl of black cats
your voice of sin
still twist
just under my skin
the scabs pick themselves open
again and again

my dreams of sunset orange
fell with the stars
spinning out of control
time stood still
as the accident unfolded
I forgot to buckle

your mask of violet
hung upon the mantle of my soul
turning truth into lies
the fires just died
the betrayal you disguised so well
your farewell inscribed "Welcome to Hell"

every color you sent my way
reflected the prism of my tears
the rainbows began to bleed
every shade of gray
still bleeding away
clotting my eyes
from tomorrow's sunrise
leaving chaos to rule the day
and hope
drowning in the rain
does the pain ever end?

don't blink

You left me here
picking up all the pieces
of everything left undone

you made me believe
in fairy tales
you made me believe
love fails

thought you were magic
thought we were one
now I'm static
and all alone

holding your shattered image
still in my heart
walking down the aisle
walking down the plank
this ring
becoming the weight
that took me down

my knight in shining armor
my night of darkest horror

you took my wings
burned them in the fire
along with my diaries
and everything I thought you'd be
you burned everything
including me

needing a plastic surgeon
to remove your marks
needing a priest
needing a therapist
needing to swallow
all these bitter pills
needing a magician
to put me back together
and make me whole

needing your face
your touch
your hands
to disappear
but every blink
brings you near
back from the dead
inside my head

I tried to hold my eyes open
but that's when the tears come
eventually, I have to blink

your living photo
just behind these curtains
reading your lips
with every wink
telling me to come closer
into the fire
with you

Only the light
can erase you
climbing up this staircase
with eyes stapled open
Father forgive me

Free

Falling

into

the

Light

where angels never blink

when angels scream

pouring concrete into my tear ducts
trying to pave a way
for bravery
but only trickles of fakery leave their fossils behind

rancid tears and cottage cheese milky eyes
leave a museum of treachery
another stain in this diary
another exclamation point
dragged out of bounds

becoming a pendulum to the music box of society

going to hide myself
in your dreams

you'll wear my eyes
of knowing
maybe you'll keep your sanity longer than I
but soon enough
you'll lose your mind
and mine will become a ghost
coming back
to haunt my former self

it'll reach for the pharmacy behind my bathroom mirror
it'll reach for the knife upon the kitchen sink
it'll learn to tie knots and learn to hang ropes
but it will never stop trying to kill itself
when ghosts wish for death

exhumed

I was brushing my teeth this morning
brushing my hair
when I looked through the air
between me and the mirror
hiding just behind my eyes
was the future
of all my past lives

I blink
and run with them
a soundtrack of piano keys
plays melodically
as I shadow my twin
but they do not recognize me
and kick me out

back in front of the mirror
watching my future
pass before my eyes

so I close them again
and turn them off
twist my hair in knots
stain my teeth with bitter cream
brush my fist into the mirror
my flesh shatters
my blood scatters
splatters
falls
drips
yet these voices remain
open my eyes brushing insane
with drops of pain

upon the walls stained
with past lives initials carved
using finger for self portrait
I draw a brush upon an empty shelf
dead hair clogging the sink
dead teeth paling to pink
and one shard of glass
bleeding from one edge
a time capsule
from all my former lives
former tenants saying goodbye
former convicts singing they're free
evicting me from my own house
trapped in the past
a ghost of the future
not able to cauterize this suture
I fly into the ethereal skies
like ashes into the wind
a personal titanic
with no lone survivor
no last tale
just a wisp of smoke
and one drop of blood
fading away
complete

never did get the message
they all tried to send me
note to self
beware
of self

so now I read this through your eyes
and me and your muse
begin to giggle
just behind your vision

floating

I wore brightly colored clothes today
to hide the freshly picked scabs of yesterday
wearing a different mask today
to hide the pain I try and bury
walking in circles inside my inner playground
there is nowhere to run
the boogie man lurks behind every corner
with family reunion eyes
it's all black and white
when your soul is nailed to the floor

an empty bed with sacrificed bears
a teddy piñata stuffed with bitten nails
walking paths in rusty creaking floor
too scared to speak
frightened by the unknown
afraid to go outside
stay in the corner and cry
hit the rewind button
pause the backstabbing
and watch
the innocence
torn from my eyes
again and again

tears of icicles
encased in glass
the cold makes everything harder
flopping in bitter white powder
making angels of death
frostbit with pain

swimming under ice
the air is always just out of reach
they say time heals all wounds
but it can't tear down the walls of eternity stone
alone
between spring and winter
in between
past and future
a wall of glass
that only I can see
but never break through
a dead goldfish in stained glass methylene blue

everyone knocks, but forgets to feed
I couldn't take the pounding anymore
I couldn't breathe the lies anymore
I couldn't live here anymore
in this
My aquarium of sewer water

the mark of a question

I saw you
hiding behind the Christmas tree lights
the branches from your heart were dry
and brittle
blinking eyes hollow
someone turned off your light
before you learned to count
hell was the unopened present the reaper left
dressed as Santa clause
lace ribbons, tourniquets and bleeding
the venom
bitten before you were seven
the clock ticks six
and page by page
you relived the horror
from chapter 5
You couldn't walk with broken legs
so you crawled
to a stop
3 years old
and the devil made you into a woman
The evil gates were somehow unleashed
eighteen months on life support
ninety days of smiles
and then the darkness
your birthday
a life in Hades
nine months in questions womb
and the only fire that burned
was the hand of God
wishing you hadn't left so soon

may I have this last dance

In the crib
with one black eye
must have done it to myself

Crawling
with a black eye
think I tripped

Walking
with a black eye
I'm so clumsy

Playing
with one black eye
fell off my bike

Limping
with a black eye
damning and cursing the sky

Wedding band
two black eyes
silent broken cries

Born into this world with a black eye
wonderering if the Grim Reaper's scythe is more gentle than
Life's fist

Tried to dance, but it only brought rain
last dance in this freeway now
ending the pain

Dreams Imprisoned in Grey Matter

People stare at me through a glass of shadows
They analyze, hypothesize, then criticize
Their answers are only problems for me
Tormenting my soul with lifeless iniquity
The shadows whisper, as I choke to swallow
This echo of laughter, so cold and hollow
My mind is chained between stainless steel posts
They raise their arms, and join in a toast
A child screams, and the people scatter
Predator and prey, join in laughter
The madness cackles and infects my soul
It screeches and crawls towards my innermost light
Tears at my eyes and rips out my sight
I jerk and writher in agony and pain
As I enter the world of mentally insane
They smile and wait, as time goes by
Then grab my soul, and wave goodbye.

solitaire

They took my belt
then shoelaces
just in case
I might do something
horrible
but they forgot about the concrete walls

like an R-rated movie
or nightmare
I found myself there

they were trying to find me
amidst the voices
but I wasn't there
somewhere behind the stare
somewhere

I don't know who killed that family
but it wasn't me
not really
you've got to believe me
Yes, those were my hands
and I remember the knife
guilty
but something's taken over me
possessed my body
it wasn't me
not really
call it insanity
but it wasn't me
who killed that family

I don't care if you believe me
just put me out of my misery
kill me
do it now
I'm begging you please

Can't you see?
He's lying to you
Can't you see?
That's not my voice
Can't you see?
That's not my laugh
and now the walls are colored in red
again

They took my belt
then shoelaces
just in case
I might do something
horrible
but they forgot about the concrete walls

negative energy

The monsters were hiding under the bed
the bed was hiding under his thoughts
behind a sheet of skull; the grey matter grew dull

the living room became the panic room
the scent of ghosts rolled in from the kitchen
and would not allow themselves to be forgotten

the seeds were thrown in dark locked rooms
without the light
fear fed the roots

the Venus fly traps pollinating lust
escaped the nocturnal prisons
and crawled into the light of young girl's prisms

hands of charm lied with deceit
convulsing
the spirit rejected its body

his heart became a graveyard
and every sin came back to haunt him

the pain became a chain wrapped around his leg
running in circles
the priest could not exorcise the demon
himself

living in the past
he became a ghost
rattling his chains

Suicidal turtles

I love you
Please remember these words...
Hopefully by this letters end
You'll all understand
Never thought it would come to this, so not sure where to
begin...
Some of this might not make any sense, but I guess I'll start
with this

The drugs weren't working and the doctors didn't know what
to do

You'll have to walk in my shoes
I wish you could feel what I do
If only you could get inside of my head
This haunted house of mind filled with ghosts and cobweb
Hollow, dark, broken and utterly empty
But I wouldn't wish that on my very worst enemy

Traveling down the road of despair and autobiographies litter
My tour guide of Fate has led me lying here
Amidst my new found friends
Evicted from broken homes and boxes
Found myself lost... hitch-hiking down the Blvd of Broken
Dreams
Couldn't find any takers...
You know how some wear love on their sleeves?
Well, it seems my sleeves are checkered pasts of paranoia and
insanity
Only one creepy guy, ever offered me a ride
Sometimes I would catch him stalking me and I'd hide
A frightening thought, a taxi converted hearse
And the driver's eyes, his stare as an octopus

A skull donned in black, wearing a long valet cap

I've read life's instructions... how you're supposed to turn
lemons into lemonade
But this life became the hammer
smashing every light bulb dreamed in my head

The light of hope a flickering dim
My fireplace of passion gone out... as even faith tries to sneak
out
Rest in peace
Now the mantel above my heart

Rest... peace
Not even sure if those words are in my dictionary anymore
Pain... hell evermore
Every synonym for love and beauty
Have become only antonyms to me

I know some have said that when you take your own life
There is a lake of fire to pay
But right now, it's my golden ticket
To Wonka's chocolate factory

Anything is better than this
Chained down in the bottomless dungeon of my being
My head being filled with voices
Each voice a tortured voice
Fading to oblivion
A part of me screams out as I hopelessly watch
Myself being stretched on the rack
My owns hands turning the crank
Me the victim
Me the inquisitor

Once thought the voices were from demons and devils

Just realizing now, they were my own consonants and vowels

My Neverland, a mindless land
A soul less land
A barren wasteland
No Tinkerbelle angel to take my hand

And my angel?
Well, my guardian angel never did pay heed to Mr. Wimple's advice
Letting this world Squeeze my spirit tighter and tighter into life's vice

Parts of my memory play only in clips of black and white
Grainy recollections of Jack Daniels on the TV stand
A hand full of pills and .38 caliber in hand
Not sure who found me

But found myself checked into one of Alfred Hitchcock's stories
Waking up in the Psycho manor, bookmarked shower scene

Seems my arrival came on Ash Wednesday
No ashen cross fingered across my head
Just a couple of numbers printed over my patient uniformed chest
Arriving with red carpet and personal limo
Then not knowing, what special occasion called for a straight-jacket
Exchanging name for a number like a convicts
Imagine how I felt reading 666

It was a lot like church there, just different rituals
I was indoctrinated early, the power of the higher dosage

Promised redemption and salvation

Baptized by medication

They took me down
Down to the depths of murky water
I suffered the bends
And still
I have yet to catch my breath
My last bubbles even now, as I try to recall
Every day, walking down that comatose hall
Every day was Sunday where we received daily communion
A handful of pills became my wafer
With some drops of water for wine
Plus 10 cc's of Valium injected IV line
The priests here are all costumed in white
And yes, the nurses are nuns and just as strict
Their tongue depressors becoming my crucifix
Checking under tongue
Swallowed my daily fix
No capsule residue here
As I gobble them like a fat boy eats cake
It's my only escape
These little pills of green and blue
Reds and yellows, and some split in two

Seems all these voices in my head
Really were demons from the dead
They performed their exorcisms upon me
No Latin incantations needed to set me free

A water filled sponge inside my mouth, my only holy water
And a priest reading from his psychiatry bible
Electro shock therapy
You don't even know

Had the recorded sessions played back for me
Could have swore I was speaking tongues

From strained and raspy lungs
Garbled words that sounded like foreign gibberish
With intermittent spaces of, 'Oh God please help me!'

That's all I understood
Seems the doctor's resident
Was ready for the priesthood

The Holy Roman Mental Church
Wouldn't be complete without an inquisition
Hands and feet, body quivering with amps
A controlled epileptic seizure
If I was a monkey, maybe PETA would have saved me

My hospital bed with arms of iron
Becoming my rotisserie pole
Waves of electric fire flowing all around me
Can't they see I'm burning...?
Just another case study
The name on my chart
'Just another nut case'

Most of the time I would wake up dreaming
How that little light in the cornered right
Next to my bolted metal cage door encased in white
Would become the shining Star of Bethlehem at night

I don't remember claiming to be Jesus or the Messiah
But here come the three Magi
Only bearing bad news
Time to stir the stew

But not with Gold, Frankincense or Myrrh
Try a heavy dose of liquid lithium
That would make an elephant eyes blur
As I begin my words to slur

Holy mother, Mary of grace
Holy Shit, my brains been maced

Seeing the lights of angels even now
Feeling like one of those little boys and how
The priests raped me too
They raped my mind
Penetration
Violation
Disintegration
My mirage left barren
My imagination iced
I could see, but now I'm blind
Walking in zombie frame of mind

Certified crazy... got my master's degree
In paranormal psychiatry

Cap and gown ready to graduate
But just like prison
Gotta meet the parole board
Time to articulate

Odd, how this insane asylum has become my acting studio
'Yes, I'm fine now sir. The voices are all gone.'

Saying my lines with so much conviction
Oliver Stone would offer me an audition

So many sleepless nights,
Instead of talking in my sleep
I would scream and yell
My confession booth a white padded cell

'Father, forgive me, for I have sinned'
Except I don't know what sins I've committed

To be committed

Trapped somewhere between heaven and hell
Living in purgatory, paying my penance
For not being strong and brave like everyone else

Keep your chin up, tomorrows another day
Take your vitamins and remember to pray
Cliché quotes from the book of 'Life for Dummies'

I am an empty hole
I am only a shell
Living in hell
My fractured steps have led me here
Cold concrete my final bed
With sheets of painted rectangles

Where most see road kill
I feel the wind is still
Except for the rushing
Of my angels of 18 wheels

Here at the end now
My last secret now being told
I was so weak and helpless
I did finally take that one offered ride

Leaving no legacy behind
Just an empty chalk line
Scattered across Northbound 1011
Climbing my turtle-shelled stairway to heaven
I love you
Remember me...

sleepy dreams

They know

The sun has moved to the other side
the stars are shining bright tonight
upon telephone poles 30 feet up
casting their beams upon me
Feels like someone
somebody
is watching me
catch the rearview mirror
no one glancing backwards
Take the keys and begin the journey

through their telescopic lenses
they see my every step
zoom in close
think I hear the question
'Did he shave today?'

The doors open
like an automatic mouth
a feeling of uneasiness tingles the spine
as old wrinkly eyes stare straight through UV protection
into my red eyes
behind the curtains
and into my very soul

'Put up a wall
Don't think of anything'
I say to myself
out loud
Walking past and looking ahead
the eyes burn holes in shirts thread

Someone's talking to me
but can't tell who
look up at the half dark moons
everywhere
wondering whose watching me
and is it one, two or three
someone has got to check the dressing rooms
What do they look like
and what do they see
do they see me
staring back at them?
Am I a suspect now?
are all cameras on me now
on every screen
monitor
like some crazy movie
they are all watching
I can feel it
but there's not enough protection
or acting skills
to pull this one off
Trying to act normal
while everything moves fast forward
room temperature at maximum speed

a stranger walks by
glances at me
wonder who that is
are they watching me too?
a spy perhaps
clever disguise
Nice shoes

the cashier gives me the evil eye
as I try to un crinkle my unlucky dollar bill

shove it into her mouth
then wait for the change

can't wait to get out of here
a few more steps
when the alarms go off
'Intruder
Intruder
Halt
Stop'

a herd of footsteps
followed by grabbing monkey arms
check my bags
check my receipt
Tell me I'm free to go
Wonder if that is how they got my fingerprint
Free to go
as they watch me leave
from their castle walls
gazing from the stars
30 feet above

Turn the key and leave
behind
a car is following me
wonder if they are controlling the lights
they seem to stop only for me

unlock the door
pick up the phone
911
almost
they are probably in on it too...
better to lay low
the loud cranky beep

hang the phone up
look into the mirror
and suddenly realize
I'm still wearing paranoid eyes
it was just another trip
to wal mart
another filled prescription
a glass of water
bitter pills
I gently close my eyes
then gently press against my lids
and wait for the fireworks to die

perched upon the attic stairs

The bitter fruit of insanity hang from the branches of my family tree
With seeds of confusion and rotten cores, twisted stems and worms galore

Excuse me for a moment, while I swallow all these pills
Side effects increasing appetite
Causing me to take a bite
From the fruits of inherent insanity

In my head a storm is brewing
Perhaps I should write
No - carve into my skin
Warning Warning Tornado Warning
Perhaps you should take heed
Surely you noticed the darkened red skies becoming black in these zigzagging eyes

Waves of neurons rising and falling
Tidal waves foam across my cerebrum ocean
Category five hurricanes no levy can hold
Extreme winds with excessive hail damage
Soon destroying the foundation of relationships
No, Insurance doesn't cover forever lost friendships

The lightning storms striking upward within the grey clouds forming
Cover your ears now, can you feel the thunder bellowing
Screams and curses from my throats amplified guitar chords
No amateur here, I'll hammer and fret - conditions are ripe to perform my set

Wild fires rage across my senses plain

Torched and burnt to a feathery dry crisp
My skull multi-tasking a cigarette tray
Only carcinogens and ash remain
Migraines, tumors, epileptic seizures
Sure, there all in there
But these drugs for despair
Can't stop me from pulling out my hair

Everything's blurred slow motion now, making it more
painful to see
Where's Jacques Cousteau
To document this shark eating frenzy

A three pound wrecking ball
Left side, right side, and all squished in between
A self contained quarantine
My mind, its own CDC

So put on your masks
And strap yourselves in
Lock yourselves in the fallout shelter
For this hemisphere is helter skelter

A straight jacket for the brain
What a novel idea
But I'd prefer a total transplant
Put my name on top of that list
You think I'm kidding
I'm pleading now, begging upon my knees
I'll take a coma patient please

Call me when it's ready
Until then, I'll just wait here
With ghostly blank stares
Perched upon the Attic stairs

do you know your enemy?

I felt the knife sliding between my blades
saw your shadow
trying to slither escape
you knew I'd catch you
and still
you do
what you have always done
taking your broken shards and ripping my lung
then stare at me awhile
rip out my tongue
unable to speak
but still able to scream
I yell at the top of shredded lungs
Stop hurting me
your eyes haunt me
your words taunt me
and your voice
sounds like me spoken through broken glass

I thought of you as a twin
and perhaps
that was my sin
following a dragon
that spoke as a lamb
the beast rising from the crimson sea of my heart
the veins and rivers run red
not able to buy or sell
not able to walk, blink or bleed
frozen here
blinded here
a prisoner here
dying
wishing someone would hear

dwelling in the ice caves of loneliness
my thoughts echo off the moldy walls
the eternal halls
and you twist the knife again

my eyes are black
my wrists are bruised
never felt so alone
used
never understood the word hollow
until now
sometimes I wonder if I'm still alive
but your eyes
they remind me
as they haunt me
then follow me
as you laugh when I fall down
but you were always there
to never comfort me
to always laugh at me
to take away my tranquility
replaced my blankets and sheets
with serpents and nails

my dear evil twin
a one bodied Siamese twin
speaking three different languages
sometimes I wish
I had the strength to murder you
sometimes I wish
the world had no mirrors
it would be easier to live then
thinking that someone else
had driven that stake through my heart

not sure how to start
never knew how to end
kept my eyes off to the distance
my own little island
where the cannibal is inside

somewhere in the darkness of me
you hide
the place where fear is real
where your fingernails scrape the insides of me
my own worst enemy
me
myself, and I
perhaps one day we can all be friends
but until then...

I'll be plotting my revenge

Diary of a mad man

I want to take you to the place I know
my black heart

I want to take you to a place I call home
where all the white doves are killed by edgar allen ravens
The place I hide of murky caves in dark caverns
tied behind white curtains
Scribbling calligraphy upon suicide notes
from novocained gums
erasing tears of chalk dust
A starving artist painting Glutton's portrait
an abstract impressionist painting with blood and oil
fingernails imbedded in the darkest corner
All displayed with interrogating lights
layers of strokes all out of twisted joints
Everything looks perfect from far away

I want to take you to the place I know
where capillaries are stuffed with hungry leeches
the devil's playground

I want to take you
down my rabbit hole
show you how deep it goes
please, just hide behind me
I'll lead the way
just be sure to bring your armor and sword
There are monsters in here of flaming wings and fear
I just wanted to take you
I had to tell you
just needed to show you
in case anybody wondered
where I've been

I never promised you a rose garden

paper cut roses
wounds that weep
black feathered petals
slicing deep
past the skin
and artificial layers
piercing your soul
an empty wind howls
twelve dozen black lies
all wrapped in razor wire
holding on tighter
under your tears
drowning all the years
shedding humanity skin
eyes of sin
becoming something
you've never been
becoming a stranger
kaleidoscope tunnel vision
making your own incision
through ribs and chest
into cavity wall
where it's cold and hollow
life became the bitter pill
rather choke than swallow
blinded by hate
masquerading fate
cutting yourself open
self-mutilation
wiping your lips clean
gnawing your pain
muttering a lost song
chewing on your tongue

gargling on flesh
spitting out the present and past
a bloody wishing well
living in hell
thought you cast out the demons
but while you were sleeping
they all had children
now they are biting
now they are scratching
everything left unseen
your former self
a slice of swiss cheese
an empty chest
an empty nest
withering away
your garden of grey matter
now devoid of color
a dead layer of topsoil
where beauty cannot grow
piled with rocks
and every kind of weed
where reds and blues
become dungeon black
and what is
and what was
all draining back
into a stagnant creek
where maggots and mosquitoes
gather to breed
where the only seed
which grows upon the bank
are paper cut roses
and black feathered petals

the screams from dandelion kisses

Cotton candy memories disintegrating under the drool of
yesterday's broken promises
the yellow sky and blue birds stop singing
start screaming
then die
the true and false splattering into vomit green
and all the memories left chained
and unseen
begin to crawl and hide themselves
deeper and deeper
into the caverns of oblivion

the pain explodes like molten lava
showering everything with it
red
the color of blood once it falls upon the cold floor
like a fish out of water
struggling to breathe
fighting to stay
red
anemic and pale like vampire flesh
her nightmares on fire
the thunder and lightning
bringing blood and brimstone
hidden
behind the broken screaming
her earth quakes as her lips tremble and all the walls begin to
fall
a porcelain figurine
she imagined was herself
crashes and splinters
into a million shattered pieces
even the most precious moments

the ones she hid upon the uppermost shelf
have fallen
and all the darkness
she kept hidden from the light
suddenly crept under her eyes
becoming the birthing place of tears
her souls shadow
dripping in dead skin slack
her nerves
colored in scratches of chemical black
her heart
an empty holocaust museum
the weight of injustice crushing her spirit
hope suffocating
every bone fracturing
leaving
shreds and shards of penetrating
broken charcoal skin
bleeding ashes
she cries bloody tears within
blind eyes from dark cold hearts whisper pass
the stench of roadkill follows her with the maggots and flies
a bread crumb trail for Death to follow
the Grim Reaper
finally enters her reality
and mightily
plays His instrument of death
the scythe rising with the full moon
when suddenly
salt crystals begin pouring from His eyes
He falls to wounded scabbed knee
and silently begs her
"Will you marry me -
please?"

placing a ring upon her finger

made from the screams of broken dandelion promises
and the emptiness
from hollow birthday wishes blown dead
and everything left unsaid
'I do'
she whispered upon winter's wind
just before she grabbed the blade herself
and cut them both in two
leaving her memory behind
a ghost
to haunt the dreams
of the next Grim Reaper
to come along

motel 666

Living in purgatory
The place between the living and the dead
the place between never giving up and wanting to die
blowing truthful wishes from dandelions dragon wings
Upside down pounding kicking and screaming
trapped in Disney's new make believe - filmed live 3D
'Buried six feet under and still alive'
Narrated by the ghost of Vincent Price
Invisible man turned Frankenstein
Vampire praying to wooden stakes and holy crosses
A mummy wrapped in forgotten linens of skeleton key closet
Soaking wet in flames of regret
A dreamer marking the days in serrated Sharpies
calendar arms of blood, scars and anemic flesh
Growing older waiting for a time machine to be invented
The living dead
Zombie land

Playing yourself on Transylvania HDTV, commercial free
sitting upon a lawn of freshly cut grass and well placed
flowers
A broken down television set
making the flashes of light dance atop tombstones and graves
misty holograms taking moonlights spotlight
re runs of Lifetime horror movies, up all night
Working the graveyard shift with midnight black cats
embalming lit candles play in the background
Bones and rotting fingers making ravens fly
Eerie whispers chariot riding frost bitten breeze
Last rights, séance and last prayer unspoken
dredging up the spirits of the dead
digging up the spirits of dreams once had
unearthing all those birthday wishes hitting walls of black

splattering your back with remnants of hopeless romantic screams,
The reapers lullaby rocking you back to sleep
the cradle between the living and the dead
where goblin spiders have nightmares of you

A wandering soul trapped in time
I'll light a candle for you

null and void

Didn't want to go this time...
but something kept calling me back
down the corridor and into my soul
where everything is black
into the depths of myself
where no one else can see
searching for an answer
but never knowing the question
like playing tag with an invisible friend
and forgetting where to look
think I've been through all the rooms
but something keeps calling me back
into myself, into the black
it's on the tip of my tongue
just can't get it out
searching for something
I don't know yet
feeling alone, but not quite
thought I heard a noise
but it was only my steps
walking in a maze
when I realize
it's my heart
I've been looking for

Didn't want to go this time
but something kept calling me back
it was my heart
calling me back
but now I'm lost
forgot where it is
around in circles
back and forth again

getting tired of this game
thinking of giving up
how hard can it be
to find your own heart

Here I am
in the darkness
not knowing
where to start
perhaps it's hiding from me
perhaps I'm avoiding it
don't know which way to turn
just know
that I didn't want to go this time
but my heart keeps calling me back
where is the path
that leads to this beat
which turn should I take
but then it hit me
and I
I don't know if I can take it
a nuclear epiphany

I'm in my heart
I've been here the whole time
and it is so silent
it's empty and hollow, cold and utterly black

Wishing now that I had brought some flowers
it would have liked that
nothing left to do
but say a prayer and bid adieu
nothing left
to call me back
nothing left
it's all black

hieroglyphical mirages

I looked outside the window today
watched the invisible stars above
my mysterious dreams below
found a pack of butterflies running away
from a flock of black ravenous ravens
being chased by black storm clouds
so I ran

followed winds direction
found my tennis shoes and raincoat
began chasing after them
seeking to capture and contain

a double winged mouth flies south
falls trapped into my umbrella net
with orange sunset fuzz licking its mouth
I gently blow the magic dust
place it into my jar
the beginnings descent

tightened lid
as tightened nerves
always enough holes to breath
but never enough room to scratch
filled with all the artificial things I loved to death

make its home
just like my home
decorated with razor wire edges
and poison berry hedges
scraps of glass for bed
and every cry left unsaid
becoming my comforter

my quilt of tears
tightly woven and loosely fitted
never warming
never soft
always rough
always hard
concrete pillow head

feeling so sad
watching this poor creature
with mirror bed
trapped a dream
but never let it breath
the jar was always too black

and I watched
as the water began to fill
the every thing

its wings cut into shreds
its heart, once full of tears
ripped to shreds
finally
the creature used its tail to slice its own wrist

it said a last prayer
as a mantis should
bid the world adieu
whispered a silent song
and became goodnight

the jar falls and shatters to the earth
the lid loosens with an ironic twist
only in death, was it finally free

piercing
painful
stings blanket my cold skin
as a cloud of mosquito's begin draining within
they all fill up like helium balloons
and are led down what I thought was a parade
but ending up being a freak show charade
nailed to the wall as everyone pays their soul for a chance to
burst the balloon and win a voodoo doll
bleeding anemic dreams
the shrapnel digs into my screams
fills my eyes with sand
find my socks stuck down my throat
like a slippery eel tied in knot
my laces tied to leaches
walking in lacerated circles
walking this muddy path
this bloody path
this clotted trail of quicksand

around and round
where your souls become scabs
and your last words are scarab beetles
building a nest in your dead grey hair
the only remnant that you ever existed
lies hidden
trapped inside your pyramid shaped heart
and cursed is the one
who lets the demons out

When your eyes were tiger striped

Meow
look at me, over here
Purr
let me rub your leg
cat's in heat
I'll let you fuck me if you say you love me

cats in heat
cats in heat
buy my soul for a dove dripping in blood

cats in heat
cats in heat
sell your body for a one-night stand

someone raped your harvest
and joined trust and paranoia
hand in hand

the background screams
rises with intensity
breath becomes choked and hollow
difficult to swallow
flying too high now
just wanting to escape
just a little while
just didn't expect
to be suffocating paranoia's breath
reaping the repercussions
falling down before reaching the halfway line
flying down
now
way too soon

wondering how long this feeling will last
wondering how long it will stay
worried it's not going away

it's not going away
it's not going away
it's not going away

Illusions

Waving riddles for bait
leaving metaphors dangling
she drew me in with her succulent breath
her resonating fake smiles and shiny lying teeth
a facial contortionist filled with empty sighs
rented orgasm contact eyes
the specks of gold, were all floating in my head
dipped in tips of blackened red

"I love the way your heart breaks"

her voice recorded in prisoner recess
splattered upon my face like projectile vomit

"I love the way your blood tastes"

her tongue scraping against my back
like a home-made shank
made from barb wired lips

"I love when you're on your knees
begging please
waving
the white flag again
I am sitting here silently
watching you
struggle
to breathe again

"I love..."

she said with backwards voice
with specks of Poe and Hitchcock

"I love
watching your eyes
becoming
dirt
with every shovel poured upon your grave"

little did she know
she was speaking to my tombstone
my shadow
as I had learned to follow
my own instincts and voice
it was my ghost she was loving to death
and there she will remain
stay
chained
the shell of my former self
becoming her home
a hermit crab
my beautiful bride
the life in her eyes
died
and all those specks of gold
were finally out of my head
now I am free
watching the sunset
the birds sing
and her
only a memory
cracked open and rotting somewhere in the nest of a dead
fallen tree
under the canopy
of a weeping willow
shaped and manicured
by the hands of forbidden love
with Cupid's broken arrows and almost lover dreams

flavors of ash

I gave her my heart
and she yanked it out of my chest
she took all the shades of red
love
pierced them with poisonous residue
with dry scales and broken fingertips
she folded everything I gave her
it
over and over
placed it above her candle of darkness
and burned
tossed the ashes with some monkey blood
dipped the tips in carnivore black
mixed it with two rabid bat fangs
wrapped the whole thing with black widow web
ground it all into a powder
then lit it on fire
and the smoke
rose higher and higher
until it reached the nostrils of heaven
causing the clouds to rip and tear
sending black showers of apathy
polluting the lands
all the flowers
smell of ashes
all the rainbows
have turned to grey
following the lizards into charles darwin dreams
trapped somewhere in this inky mire
is a butterfly
struggling to stay afloat
and all the mutant ants are working together
to preserve the gold flavored butter

my grave marker

Lips of strychnine
glossy shine
Voice of nectar
spoiled turpentine
Acid fumes
Your breath
the kiss of death
Slithering snake fingers
creeping
constricting
Electrical cord arms
strangle angel prayer
Poisonous hair
intoxicating
luring
suffocating
Locks of black leeches
eclipse sacred light
Lashes of bat wings
dipped in liquid black
From eyes of strawberries
and lips of cream
To
Eyes of night
and midnight screams
Neck laced in candy
Cotton candy ear
bittersweet ecstasy
Horns protruding there
Valentine heart
draped in vampire cape
Ebony top and bottom
overlade

Silky ivory skin
Chocolate and vanilla
double dip
Banana split
My Sweet tooth
betrayed me here
Inside the dragon's lair
barred shut
barbed metal gates
My tombstone
unknown graveyard
As a single cherry
you now sit
My coffin
your desert
Crow cackling
Spider Laughing
Silent leaf falling

the sound of you
the sound of me

The Wind
The Sea
The Sound Of You and Me

The Fire
The Ice
Slowly Melting
Drowning You
Drowning Me

You were Lost
I was Found
The Fiery Crash
Our Beating Sound

Heaven Above
Hell Below
Us in Between
A Love Unseen

You the Flood
Me the Drought
A Muddy Mixture
Of Faith and Doubt

I Possessed Wings
You the Horns
White Fire and Black Ice
You were the Sickness
I was the Cure
Darkness and Light
Hope and Fear

Blindness and Sight

I Was The Oil
You The Water
The Pain and The Peace
Invisible Dreams Ceased

Summer and Winter
Colliding Together
Snowflakes of Acid
Snowmen of Plastic
White Christmas
Black Halloween
Holy and Profane
Sin Striped
Candy Cane

Impure Love
Pure Hate
Beauty
The Bait

The Predator
The Prey
Eyes of Angels
Lured Away

A Voice so Gentle
A Kiss so Tender
Lips so Sweet
Your Mouth
A Sharks
My Heart
Your Red Meat

The Wind
The Sea
And the Sound
Of Your Teeth
Crunching on Me

Devoured
By
The One
I
Love

The Sound
Of
Silence

The Sound Of You
And Me

And Now You are Standing
And Now I am Lying
Six Feet Between Us
Me Holding a Rose
You Holding a Shovel

The Sound Of Dirt
Covering
Me

The Sound of Breath
Suffocating

The Sound of Peace
Bleeding

The Sound of Laughter
Crying

The Sound of a Rainbow
Imprisoned

A Silent Echo
The Sound
Of You
And Me

The Sound of Shadows

The Sound of the Scythe

The Sound Deceased

The Sound of You and Me

The Sound
of
the End

shipwrecked

the twilight beckons the blood to rise
the seas are roaring pain again
crashing against broken backs
boulders crashing on shattered shoulders
Holding your breath and gripping on tight
it's an everlasting night
where the waves are rising but never falling
crashing on raw exposed severed nerves
the moon is howling for the sea to rise
the tide that comes with laugh and wicked song
the sandcastles are all breaking down
dreams becoming smithereens
dragged into the tempest with watery screams
the echoes are circling like evil vulture sharks
creating a thunder and a mist
a whirlpool sucking like vampire
a black hole taking your soul to hell

where your inner demons play darts with your voodoo doll
inside outside and everything twisted upside down
throw you in the trash and dare you to dance
you've become the candle upon death's birthday cake
and all your demons are wishing you away

stayed in the dark too long
held your breath too long
talking to shadows, becoming a ghost
you waited too long, you held on too long
and now you are gone
alone
stranded
a sunken vessel of empty treasure

7, 8, lay them straight

Flipping memories like pages between the day and night
lost lotteries autumned the falling sky with burnt leaves
trailing black and white
the ashes buried the lost chapters under stone walls and
freshly dug graves
names
places
forgotten and erased
locked up in a cage
clipped wings
and never taught to speak
of these things
the monsters of the deep

these voices
they whisper when no one is looking
the cracking of broken spines
and screams of pain
prisoners
held hostage
in the lost chapters of my mind
lost chapters frozen on the dark side of the moon
where my subconscious secretly hid them
disguised under shadow of grief and horror

I stared at the pages against a mirror
torn and dirty
blank and weeping
emotions bleeding ink smudged the skeleton keys and puzzle
edges
a riddle with no smile
leaves no trail
nor tears to follow

in the twilight hours I prayed
breathed the pages before me
grinding their fired edges violently against my anemic palms
the ashes blew down my nose and into my soul
lighting a tiny fire that echoed off the mossy cave
a voodoo doll passed before me
looking just like me
then a darkness
and a fear
going deeper
where the haunted voices scream for release
to be seen
to be remembered
to rise from the dead

Dear Diary
'Why did you betray me?'
Dear Diary
'Why doesn't anyone help me'
Dear Diary
'Who am I?
and why are all these pages empty before me
written in braille by yesterday's bleeding footsteps
Chapters seven and eight
they escaped
I hear their howls and taste their stench consuming the air
with vengeance upon growling lips'

so I dove into the ocean
and locked all the doors and put out the light
some things are better left
forgotten
buried and undisturbed
in the abyss
alone

where angels never tread
and lost chapters
never uncover lost treasures
only skeletons
and sharks
the demons of the dark
their voices never cease
when no one is looking
you'll hear them
again and again
rattling their chains
chapters seven and eight
don't make the mistake
they escaped
and their appetite for vengeance
cannot be quenched
the demons of the dark
chapters seven and eight
seven
and eight
they escaped
'Dear Diary
my final entry'

Dear god please help me!

shatter and thyme

choking on sarcasm
said you were joking
but your face is telling
* a different story*
than the words you played
said it wouldn't hurt (hiding the band-aids)
but I should have known
by the promise in your voice
silent alarms bells ringing
left a knife spinning
(spinning)
like my head
all pinched in knots
left a knife (bleeding)
bleeding
the trail begins and ends with you
Us

Fate playing matchmaker was never Destiny's child
opposites attract and I'm supposed to love you
mind whimpers, I need a bodyguard from you
a protector
some kind of barrier
the invisible one
the physical one
becoming two in one
a marriage made in heaven
sealed in hell
but the ring fit perfectly
and you said your vows
I remember the laughter
and distant howls
I recall the warmth upon your skin
your cold toes

wearing the same clothes
your long hair told me to stay
when I should have ran away
brown eyes of innocence
nudging me to look upward
you played Taps on piano
as it fell upon me
crushing me
you take a bow
reach down with your smile
try to smother me
I cried and you giggled
always erasing me out
an equalizer of neutral chained together

traveling canyons beside me
we come to a Y in the road
looking back at the same time
wondering
if this is deja vu
all over again
taking the wrong lanes
always the same
thorns and stings
while you ride piggy back
until finally
here we stand
both together, hand in hand
upon the edge of a cliff
how can I trust you now, after so many betrayals

seems to me
it's time
to take the hammer
to all these mirrors

day old hate

chewing the tasteless gum of regret
blowing bubbles of sores
biting tongues
bleeding lips

Following the breadcrumbs thrown by the wayside
thought I was making my own trails
blazing my own paths
only to find
circular pain
in between the ruts and scabs
everything so eerie
stuck in this place of day old hate
deja vu reigns over again

dancing feet in motionless move
severed hands writing left handed again
reading the book with Babylonian breath
trying to cover the scents of decay
burying the sins of yesterday

last rites and sacrificing rituals
burning my favorite songs
under the oaths and ashes of blood
the music in your voice
is out of tune tonight

your eyes aren't the way I remember drawing them

black and hollow
a pair of raven's eyes
reflecting a mirror up to my soul
this picture

isn't the way I remember it
everything is out of focus
a tombstone in between us
painted in water colors
upon a canvas of tears
Your smile

what happened to your smile?

your bloody mouth resembles a trap

weeping statues

Reading quotes in brail upon sandstone memorials
scent of dead fish rolling waves
columns of crumbling intellect
The ghost of Plato
twisting Aristotle's chains
nuclear whispers from Socrates
speaking riddles hypocrisy

Every step moving farther backwards
hallways of broken footprints
the stairway to hell's maze

Broken fingered memories
over the darkness covering keys
single thoughts as single notes
playing over and over again
water tortured brain

Violenced neurons lightning
cobra venom striking
acid drops keep falling on my head
only yellow ribbon is jugulars tourniquet

Just a scarecrow
stuffed and smiled
the crows lining my sleeves
black demon thieves

Stealing every morsel
capturing every thought
slurping the rain before cracked lips
black winged covered eyes
impaled upon doubt and nailed with fear

Would settle for one angel and demon in each ear
pulled the shortest straw
the pool of satan's synchronized swimming team
two footed halloween christmas tree

Stop dropped and rolled
burning scars of fool gold
tangled and mummified
SOS on hieroglyphical wall
Entombed in puppet strings
bed of Scarab beetles
silken tarantula bed sheets
black widow's goodnight kiss

Stop dropped then died
becoming the last tear
fleeing the scene of this accident

Torn

listening to the voices
trying to make sense of it all
the darkness and light
mingling their music
trapped in cemetery flesh
my spirits wings have been folded
chained and clipped
wanting to fly
but having to die
searching for truth
in maze of false light
wondering why
the sky is blue in light
wondering why
the sky is black at night
awake during the day
sleeping at night
when the angels and demons
wrestle and fight
a walking mansion
with boarded up windows
afraid to take the wrong turn
but it's the only way to learn
sometimes walking backwards
sleeping upside down
praying out loud
from a Ouija boarded heart
looking inside
a shattered piece of art
put on the auction block
darkness raises the stakes
then plunges them all inside
ties another knot

adding to the weight
added to the menu
roasted heart
a la carte
clotted wine
and salted rim
a sacrificed pig
with human skin
shredding and ripping
in this vortex of sin

tis the season

Black cats screeching
hairy spiders creeping
invisible footsteps creaking
hidden shadows speaking
Unseen eyes burning holes
goblins whispering ears
lying in bed
wide awake
can't sleep
can't walk
cannot day
cannot dream

Just a tanned hide
flapping in the wind
Cut, hollowed then stuffed
with soft metal screams

The year where time began dying
everything in slow motion
The clock blinking 9:11
A birthday cake of grinded organs covered in rotten cheese
maggots the candles as buzzing flies yell 'surprise'
Shadows sing songs of last rites
Open handwritten card
intrigued the writing matches mine
one word
Die

Another visit from Cupid's evil twin
sending Valentine flowers of Emily Rose
with scented poison and corpsed thorns
wrapped in fiberglass coffin

a love note, written in wicked jagged lines
Fuck you

The season matching my heart and skin
Christmas time filled with empty boxes
A dead tree in stagnant waters
celebrating alone
with raw dough and curdled milk
making a noosed wreath of hanging sheets
Hanging above a cold fireplace of ashes
a suicide note upon a sticky reminder pad

Halloween finds its way
a demented holiday for a cemented soul
trick or treat 24/7
Rotten apples and sour candy
nougat of gunpowder topped with caramelized strychnine
no need for ghosts and scary cats
just my heart, in shades of black

Where all the windows are nailed shut
and the only door leads to the morgue

shadows luck between karma and fate

The pain, that travels
with every day's footstep
The rock in your perpetual shoe
traveling in time with you
from cabbage patch to end of the train tracks
it's the itch under healed skin
the pain that travels through time
every footstep and tear dropped

The lightning striking from heart to brain
smoke and fire
screeching wheels
sparks and flame
The train of pain
running the traveling tracks of time
collision coursed dead end
when highway's memory intersects scarred lane
where the past lives in darkly veiled fairy tales
under subcutaneous layers of thick skinned books
binded in a healed ever-bleeding wounded scar
Band aid CPR
Gangrene Neosporin
Infectious memories diseasing through time
every step taken
every tear forsaken
every hole crawled into
every kiss denied
every handshake's cold twist

Scars fester pools in the cold dampness of darkest drools
explorer turned cave dweller with bats of familiar masks
The pain which sails from winter to summer
cutting cold ice's thunder

Floating under hushed whispered words never spoken
only written and read with mind's eye
The insatiable migraine never cured
from blood cells of cancered memory
flowing through clotted heart beats
and pale gasping breaths

It's the sorrowful glance downward
staring below from towered walls and imprisoned souls
The pain from guardian angels demon possessed
It's the pain that travels with you
The reflection no one can see but you

'mirror, mirror... on the wall'

Does the pain ever end?

empty chambers

Clutching four leaf clovers
White knuckles trembling
5 empty chambers
one hollowed point
Holy water from temple
Baptizing cold steel

Forgive me father
For I have sinned

Click
Click
Click
Click
Click

Challenging Fate
I roll the die
Snake eyes
Deathly eyes
The Reapers scythe ascends
Upon my knees
I rest my head upon the guillotine
A Grim smile
One candle remains
I make my wish
The sun is eclipsed
The curtains drop

Four dead clovers
Spray painted red
Four empty chambers
Hollow and still

falling backwards

I threw my head under water and screamed
but the fish didn't care
I pulled out my hair and breathed
but I couldn't find the air
so I picked up the pieces I was left holding
polished the dirt, until it was golden
putting the puzzle back together
it resembled my better half
but when I looked again
it became a golden calf
only one part was missing
so I gave it a heart
but then the whole thing just melted
and when I opened my eyes again
I was inside an Egyptian pyramid
staring into a sarcophagus
I read the hieroglyphics
the names of both of us
on the wall I saw
you
driving a chariot
and I was pulling it
with a smile on my face
then the image erased
and we were both on an island
thought it was heaven
until I saw the poison
smeared across your lips
and behind the mascara
a laugh
that only madmen should cackle
so I ran to the ocean
began swimming
thought I was free

until my memory
became a shark
chasing after me
the last thing I remember
were the black eyes
and that one time
I awoke from my sleep
and found you staring at me

so cold it burns

I knew it was a dream
so I didn't dare pinch me
saw you there
standing
looking
you were lost
and I knew
my open eyes were your escape
so I willed myself deeper
and began building a cage

you didn't seem startled when I approached
like you knew something
but you weren't telling
so before anything
I gazed into your eyes
saw past the blue
behind the stare
a gateway to deja vu

I saw you there
standing
and I knew it was a dream
just seemed
like it keeps happening
over and over
and every time I wanted you more
needed
define lust
then place us between
that's how it seemed
I remember it was only a dream
and I never wanted to wake up

it was you
standing there
looking lost
I looked into your eyes
a heightened awareness
an exhale
biting lips
and then our kiss

the tension released with the sound of a trap

then something snapped
and I saw you there
looking at me
lost
standing in a cage
crying
but your eyes
were wide open
and you were pinching yourself
over and over again

again and again

you were the bow that played the strings of my heart so
beautifully
you lit all the candles
upon this dark and stormy sea
Your eyes were the fairest of them all
and all your smiles became the stars that spoke to me
you know Capricorn will always be my favorite
and how you bit
your sweet pink lips

we were the secret note inside the message in a bottle
sailing upon the dreams of clouds
and rising above the wings of angels
the world was dying all around us
but the power of two
was something dark earth could not undo
have I told you lately
how much I love you?

from classical and sensual
to rock n roll
your fingers pushed all the keys
you were so good for me
Do you remember trying to break all the records
for the longest kiss
the deepest kiss
the wettest and most sensual kiss
the kind that numbs your lips and tongue
and makes your hair stand up and salute
your adrenaline became a drug that's addictive
when the energy in your eyes
is the only thing that gets me so high
Yes, I will always remember

now someone call Guinness
because I think we've finally done it
the Moonlight Sonata
is making shadows behind a sunset umbrella

the sharks are gone and the sun is dawn
let's take another dip
baby, we're not done yet
all these years were just the beginning
we were never meant to say goodbye
and that's why
our lives are in a state of chaos and nothing seems normal
all these stains will not come out
a comatose state of shock
because you closed your eyes
and fell back down to heaven
I'm afraid I've lost you
I can't see you anymore
and the only memory I remember
is too painful to conjure up again
and so I'll close my eyes again
and scream your name again
I'll pray to God one more time again
and one more day will pass again
but when tomorrow comes again
I will pray again and again
because I have always loved you
right from the beginning
and this time I'm not losing you
this time I'm fighting
and I will find you
again
believe me
I will find you
and we will run into each other's arms like some kind of
foreign film

our tears and hugs will do the signing and speaking
and between the laughter and screaming
under the waterfall of tears
I'll pick you up and carry you home
here in my heart
you will never be alone
here in my arms
you can once again
sleep
and dream again
and all the colors that died inside of you
will let you breathe again
Love again

I miss you
again

somewhere inside the shadow

crossing paths with land mined bridges
crossing oceans and atmospheres
the face of love
forever sought for
always hidden behind darker veil
always absorbing the darker of things

her lips
you've traced them before with finger and tongue
sniff the air for a scent

behind closed doors a memory is unlocked
just bits and pieces like some storybook flipping pages
you find yourself
on page 41
just a glimpse
your hand in my hand

her fingertips move
you trace them with your eyes
you've seen them before
their prints
memorized
she draws a secret
you wink without thinking
answering the riddle's key
and suddenly both of your pendants start to glow
as silent explosions, the epiphany's drop

staring into each other now
inhibitions lying in the shadows
in the shadows
lying comfortably in front our vision

our eyes cross as paths
our hearts become the bridge
your voice leads me on
into your song
two captured birds
in a cage of temporary
frozen
hidden
behind a veil darker than the air

no one else can see
when we
walk into each other's eyes
and dance in the middle

it was always meant to be
you
and me

it was always meant to be
a secret
hidden
just behind the veil

forsaken

you can't see me
but I'm right here
next to you
whispering in your ear
that soft tickle you feel
it's a strange sensation
like the color of deja vu
thought I saw you in my dreams
so I closed my eyes
imagining I was here
with you
you can't see me
but you breathe me in
think you can feel me
feel like a ghost
don't want to startle you
so how do I tell you
that I am here
with you
right now
beside you
whispering in your ear
that soft tickle you feel
it's me
whispering into your ear
when I close my eyes and think of you, I'm there with you
beside you
It's not a dream
it's real
I cannot prove it
for when my eyes open
I lose it
everything gets lost and blurry

so I close my eyes
and live as a ghost
sharing my life with you
thought I had lost you
I was afraid
I was insane for a bitter time
blacker than depression
colder than ice
further into the abyss
lost - frozen - numb
anemic
silent
everything was dead
but then
I found you
in the darkness behind the veil of reality
and now I am staring at you
touching your eye lashes
trying to make you blink
I know it's only a tickle
but I cannot help but tell you
I love you
in the night time
that's when I lose you
as you bounce around the universe
all I can do is dream with you
touch your hair
touch your skin
your lips and fading perfume
kiss your ever essence
touch the fading lines upon your finger
a once upon a time wedding ring
a bright angelic voice calls my name
and I feel I'm drifting further and further away
a bright light
so I fight the angels with my screams

staying away from the others
alone now
even here in heaven
I close my eyes
searching for you again
seems there are some tears
that can never be wiped away
some memories
that can never be forgotten
and a love
that remains
a wound
hidden
a forsaken memory
bleeding
forevermore

Breaking down

I know you're there
I know you're lost
somewhere
I know you're there
somewhere
behind this layer
I know you're there
I know that stare
but I'm here
I'm right here
I know that stare
I know
that you can't see me here
I know
my words sound empty
behind this medicated layer
mumblings that make no sense
worried expressions upon your face
I know you're scared
but I'm right here
wishing you could see me
behind glossy eyes
prescription haze
I know those tears
I've shared your fears
but I'm right here
if only you could
if only you could
see me here
but you're not there
you're not there
somewhere
past your pity

I know
you would see me here
shining my light
hoping you would find me
hugging you tight
even though I know
I'm just an after thought
but that doesn't stop my love from burning
from shining
for you
cause I'm right here
holding you tight
burning bright
just outside the door
of your heart
burning
waiting
breaking
down

running through closed doors

The rivers were dry
leaving canyons behind
winter came before summer could be born
dreams became ice
leaving traces of hope in fragmented mind
secret prayers fell down before betrayal's kiss
reality became fantasy as you lived in history's sunrise
the mirrors were cracked
time stood upon its knees
the batteries had died long ago
too tired from struggling to breath
raggedy ann's dress was torn
you wept together
under life's weather

I saw you hiding
whispering
shaking
I came with water and wine
tenderness kind
I've lived your life before
I know it's not pretty
believe me
I understand the misery
hypocrisy
fakery
I'm here to help you now
I will carry you
through the mud
in the fire
over fragile ice cracking under gossip's breath

I'll put to bed the rumors of past mistakes
kill every rusted snake
and every pound of regret and shame
I'll bury them together
in an unmarked shallow grave

I'll teach you how to forget
and remember how to live
we'll dance under the moon
count every rainbow
and kiss in the rain's embrace
I will cover your ears until the thunder disappears
hold you when war breaks the silence
everything you wanted
dreamt of
someone you can trust
someone who will never lie to you
someone you can hold and never let go
best friend and lover
knight in shining armor

Sleeping beauty
awake
and see me here
right in front of you
feel my heart
beat upon your chest
taste my lips
and live again
dream again
rise one more time
and try
again

ready, aim...

The whispers were in the dark
but they found a way
the shadow's feather dropped into realities still water
causing a ripple
saliva dribble
flashbacks
panic attacks
depression's tale could be heard dragging in the distant future
I tried to go under
I tried to save you
but the weight was too much to bear
I threw the circle of truth around your cynical hands
but you cut all the strands with a slice of your tongue
The whispers found bravery within shadows veil
they came out of hiding from underneath the puddle

the winds chattered their threats atop the northern
hemisphere
claws of ice to numb the heart
teeth of malicious
to gnaw the flesh

I tried to go under
but you couldn't find my soul
only the surface
you scratched and climbed
pushing me deeper under your kicking feet
I screamed and screamed
and now...
the shark frenzy
the whispering of the dark
and one final ripple

running in circles

my hand became an extension of my mind
reaching for things above the ceiling
weighing the education against reality
Libra's scale grew heavy

The questions were blown with every birthday wish candle
the spirit inside the dandelion seed grew wings
riding upon the angel of wind
carrying the message with sight and sound

Over a golden sea
the moon turned blue

The summer heat was burning the memories of spring
autumn began bleeding as the birds flew south
the snowflakes came to hide the sin of winter
the kiss of Judas parted the red sea clouds
free will threw destiny's lightning bolt
thirty silver rainbows
rained down

Mary's little lamb was white as snow
walking to the slaughter

I looked into his eyes
and became a thief

I looked at myself across the fence

one hand holding a hammer
and the other
a dead rooster

I cried into the heavens
then watched the waters melt
red birds built their nests
baby angels sang
and all the dandelions
began sprouting again

singing over winter's grave

the rose petals blew away as the ashes burned grey

Following the voice I love
to the great unknown

Waiting to start a new chapter
the Forward can wait
to attend my funeral

summer's heat rose the pitch in mercury's voice
but the kisses stood cold
and far away

winter returned
again and again
I rooted for the leaves to return
and the bleeding to stop

The thunder clapped
as the oak tree fell

but the resurrection fern
gave its children to the birds
and the memory of the fallen
made friends with magical beans
reaching up into heaven
where everything is heard
and forever written

so I climbed the stalk I had planted in my dreams
tried to take a peek into Fate's crystal ball
and saw my shadow's heart
holding my lover's hand

flashing smiles of unicorn ivory
her voice thread the needle with crimson string
and my heart once again
began to sing

Nature's Shakespearean play

There is a poem written upon my hand
Sketched and engraved
before time began
All of these lines
my unspoken rhymes
All leading to
All speaking of
You

In the twilight now
My heart understands
You cannot see your name
Written upon my hand

So I have shed my skin
And become
the Mantis
Praying
Patiently (nervously)
Silently (hoping)
Waiting (for your alluring scent)
Looking (for your butterfly wings)
To cross my path
Near enough
To catch you
And take you away

Do not fear my tender grasp
As I lay you down upon the grass
Our pulses beating lovers drum
This hand was only a map
With you, marked with an X

Buried treasure
Hidden treasure
You are more worthy than all
How long I've waited for this moment
Everyone said you were only a figment

Rest your hand into mine now
No Cinderella slipper needed
Without hesitation
we will know
When our hearts become
One

Look into my eyes and see yourself in mine
The silhouette of our hands
In the shadows from branches
Like earth's picnic quilt
Our warm palms together
Flying as one bird

Two shimmering pools of autumn
The mirrors to your soul
I've already dove in
Like a child
Not even caring how deep I go

I whisper into your ear
'I love you'
A great owl replies back 'who'
My lips to yours
I speak your name
Nature's Shakespearean play

With audience and extras
Never felt so at ease

In front of a crowd
With moths as ballerina's
Dancing to the light in our eyes
As the crickets play
Upon legs of violin

One day
These arms that cover me
May become a python's embrace
But that's the risk
I'm willing to take
Love is only for the foolish
And the brave
Me the predator and you the prey
Like a lion and a lamb
Nestling together
Our own fairytale land

Suddenly the forest is silent
Sounds like footsteps in the distance
The clouds disappear
For only a second
the moon becomes our spotlight
Funny how love can make you crazy
And see things that really aren't there

Wait! It is a spotlight
Boom!

Let this be a lesson to you all
Never wear fake antlers in the fall

magically delicious

It was raining today
so I opened the sun
thought I'd create some rainbows
but that only made it worse
all the droplets had formed into a pool
and now it is boiling
so I put my hands on my hips
SCREAM
like a tea pot
start spewing like old faithful
and everyone just walks by
sometimes casting a penny my way
but this isn't New York city
so that caught my eye
and then the rain came
wishes came true
and the pennies piled up
someone finally turned on a red light
and the whole world thought
my feet were a pot of gold
thought I was in prison
but I've never been a good speller
looks like it's a prism
and the light is shining just right
I put on my magical glasses
and everything is magically delicious
the clouds turning marshmallow bright
sparkling with rainbow magic and puffs of gold
The sky explodes into a shower of fireworks
pink hearts, orange stars and green clovers
and the cow jumped over the moon
finally coming to rest upon my spoon
sorry, I was hungry

haiku hiccups

What If's
only exist
in what could have bins

four chambers filled with powder
awaiting the match to strike
Supernova

"What is light?"
The moon asked the sun
"It is my love"

After six million fires in prison
the Nazi's were released like doves
and the Lion laid down with the Lamb

The sheep carried wooden stakes
to kill vampires, the reason they came
impaling those that didn't believe the same

my fingers were writing for my brain
sending letters without postage
through wind, storm, or rain

I took the sands of time
added some water
then built my own castle

Time

Time
slips through our hands
like water
moving as a swollen river
sweeping everything in its path
some try to ride the rapids
but they always die
too young

our dreams
the moments of sanctuary
where friends become strangers once again

our dreams
the islands of sanctuary
the bigger we dream
the father way it seems
when we reach the shore
the cannibals chase them away

the past and present leave us stranded
to the unknown future

Father Time
sometimes I wonder
if he's the grim reaper
in disguise

chess

Thrown onto the chessboard
a placenta wrapped around my neck
dripping wet
a wild horse with black breath snorted fire
and ice
the game of life

the instruction manual lay buried beneath my feet
and somewhere above my head

the pawns surrounded me in spider webbed chains
a b c d e f g
count to three
red means stop
obey your thirst
war is peace

The bishops had gone underground
witness protection programs
but the choir boys were all singing a different tune

The Queen sacrificed her loyal army
one by one
The King
left alone
looked at me with familiar clarity

He took the remaining rooks and twisted them into playing
cards
dealt me a hand, while the joker danced before the throne
unwinding a long scroll
The charges were laid against me
with a voice that seemed rather bored

the river

born in a river
where everything is moving
so fast
colliding
crashing
the tears form mud with the pain
laughter hangs a rope below the bridge
giving the lungs a pause to rest
but the hands of time
and the currents push
are way too fast

forks in the road and waterfalls
destiny twists and turns
the north star disappears
always
when the reapers scythe swings

struggling to breath
caught in the current
I hold my breath
and drift away
cause I can see the daylight
when I close my eyes

born in the river
where the trees hold their breath
watching
as we drift away
they want to get away
but only their death
will let them drift away

living in the river
learning to be a swimmer
letting myself go
to sleep
far away
where the land is soft beneath my prayer

life is a river
born to be a swimmer
some race to the finish line
hurting those trying to get by
trying to gargle and drink
trying to find the land
where the sand is soft

it's not a race to the finish line
it's about doing the best we can
the direction stays off course
but in between the night and the day
the laughter and the pain
we can close our eyes
and pray

the intellectual

Diaphanous phantasms alluding ludicrous collusion
Bellicose pacifist dreams paramour intented
Ashes of reprobated incense burning hedonistic prides
leavening
smoking, alleviating, crushing, gravity
Stentorian voices agitating
abandoned synagogues
orthodox atheists chanting sermons of apotheosis thesis
The choir's song of misunderstanding, riding the note rails of
confusion to overtures of chaos
moving through the matrix with blinding speed
words a blur yet the letters remained fixed
reading brail with wooden clubs and chopsticks from chapters
of times click
reading the signs but never knowing their intending
truth spoken in foreign languages
the island of ignorance and illiterate natives
the land of blind seers and illiterate readers
smoke screens - smoke signals
SOS
Totem poles of fecal matter
the natives circle and dance
sacrificing blood upon their altar lips of Rumor

"One day a few months ago, I came upon a nice piece of
animal dropping. I liked it and took it home with me. After a
while, I didn't like it so much. It began to smell. An
acquaintance of mine liked my piece of dropping and said the
smell didn't bother him. He offered me one of his pieces of
droppings that he had grown tired of seeing. It smelled okay
to me, so we traded. We each think we got a good deal, but we
really each just got a piece of shit."   ~Anonymous~

heaven scent

Through the meadow and into the orchard
upon golden grass with skies of rainbow.

Like the remnants of millions of dandelions blowing through
the breeze
as snowflakes dripping East to West
as if the clouds lay asleep upon the ground
they flutter like wisps of cotton dancing and twirling upward
and downward, around and around

like ballerina's pirouetting upon the cool air
hovering and floating and spinning and landing
then jumping and spiraling and swimming through the
current of winds
each striking colors in the background, like dragon tail streaks
like master artists, they brushed the atmosphere with painted
strokes of brilliance methodically and knowingly

Each on their own path, each painting their own story
each dressed in pure snow
each given a message
each given a pair of wings
The angels breathed into motion by the breath of God
A voice as the scent of flowers

These messengers of peace bring with them
faith, hope, strength, courage and understanding
Wishes granted and prayers answered, hearts strengthen and
courage renewed.
And now against the sunset, these streams of light begin to
sing
amazing notes never heard by human ear.
The postal servants of God, the messengers

They ride upon his voice...
God is speaking
Listen

elusive

I rested my pillow upon the floor
upon the ashes of postage stamps
but your postcards from France...
remained hidden
written
with an invisible pen
writing secrets upon an invisible wall
of metal and flesh
electronic
hallmark scribble

the calligraphy was camouflaged
in cold black ink
but nobody was buying it
as fantasy blurred realities mistake
and bled her pain again
so I pulled a quill of a feather
from a snow white dove
began writing love letters
without a scent
or computer code number
no trail to follow

Cupid is blind in the darkness
so I write your name in secret
on recycled paper
I breathe your essence
touch you in the Braillen silence
until the light beckons
and the pen falters
when the closet door opens

and the sun rises
or so they say
and I quietly
seal away
another day

Love, always

blessed are the poor

the sinners were casting stones at the hypocrite's back
stolen from a tomb that lay empty
the bait came with the attack
seventy times seven rung on hollow ears and recent memory
and the love they said
erased itself with every judgment thrown

the prodigal son was coming home without a halo
and the elder brother
couldn't swallow
self-righteousness dwelt in the shadow of Ego
furious memorization of scripture began flowing like a
volcano
but the Father desired mercy
not sacrifice

the younger boy fell to his knees
begging Father please
forgive me

the saints grew horns
as they rolled out the book of life
pointing here
pointing there
they tried to erase the name
but the truth was written in fiery flame

and the angels who had fallen
had their wings
given back to them

What if

What if

What if the love we give
is the love we will receive after we have died

What if the love we give now
is the amount of love we will receive in heaven

For those who loved much
they will feel loved for all eternity
kindness and compassion
being the colors of eternal castles
forgiveness is the currency
the more you forgave upon this earth
the more treasure you had stored in heaven

What if
What if we forgot to love others
what kind of eternity would that be

What if we lived a selfish life
would that be like purgatory
solitary
we reap what we sow
but none of us know
what awaits us upon the other side

So what kind of life would we live
if we knew
that the amount of love we give today
is the amount of love embracing us for all eternity

What if

Spring time

Snowflakes glide gently to the ground
They enter into my mouth, and slowly melt
Silently they fall without a sound
Touch my lips, and the cold is felt
Whispers of spring ring in my ears
The colors change from white to green
Life is reborn and covers our fears
Death is forgotten and the future is seen

Four seasons yet spring is the best
Summer is fine but the sun is so hot
Winter comes like an unwelcome guest
While Autumn helps the leaves to rot.
O Spring, my love, you are so near
You have conquered death, and erased my fear

my favorite song

Standing outside
Off balanced

Outside the kings Courtroom

singing a prayer slightly out of tune
my jaw drops to its knees
ending my song

every thing is crystal
clear and golden

in the middle of this scene grows a two headed dragon tree
olive black leaves
broken white leaves
and the truth
a flaming breath
somewhere in between

a key scented apricot reaches out to me
careful of the bee
sting and bark
part real and part fantasy
halfway inside, part way outside
a door imagines itself outside the sea

walking upon the water
the shadows never see me
the waves always listen
and the wind
becomes the guide
my former melody rains down and haunts me

touch the door handle and feel the fiery
invisible hands marble my skin
coated in evil's grin
colored in yesterday's sin

RIP
engraved outside the stone

Off balanced
Outside the kings Graveyard
mixed between the ghosts and fog
are all those who ever loved
standing outside the oak tree

they all turn and drop to their knees
and play me
my favorite song

the sound of autumn falls

Walking upon feet of ashes
walking blind
burning everything behind
the whispers of smoke try to follow me
but I'm too fast for their kind
rising with the sun and walking
burning
all day long
this fire in my heart cannot be denied
the flames in my eyes
I can no longer hide
when you look inside
I know you see my soul
so I try to cover this black hole
with a fireplace and mantle
my heat
quickly dissipates
as your icicle fingers
drip over my fiery shoulders
closer and closer
the cold becomes like fire
and your tongue of ice
becomes your every liquid desire
moving and swirling and circling and breathing
twisting and feeling
touching then kissing
the insides of your umbrella
reminding the world
that summer and winter
never rise
but always fall
the full moon rising
to watch it all

Yesterday

Yesterday, you told me I was heaven bound, but today you damn me to hell
But I am the same person as yesterday; it wasn't me who changed
Yesterday, you told me that you loved me, but today you cannot look at me
But I am here telling you, I never changed
Yesterday you said that God loved me, but today you say He hates me
And so once again I tell you, I never changed, it was you who changed

You say that it is my choice... but I tell you, I was never given a choice
God made me the way that I am, why do you question God?
You said, that God answers prayer if they are according to His will
And so I prayed, over and over and over and over again
To take this away from me, to change me... this isn't something I wanted
But He doesn't bring the change you seek... who are you to judge?
Yesterday you tucked me into bed and sang me lullabies
Today you can't stand the sight of me

Yesterday, you liked being in my company
Today, you ignored me, as if I were a stranger
Yesterday, you called me a brother, you called me a sister
But today you call me an abomination

Physically exhausted, Emotionally spent
Spiritually lost
Lost in a world that does not care about me
Lost in a religion that does not love me

Yesterday, I surrounded my heart and mind with walls
Today, God tore through the barriers I had created
Yesterday, I was living a nightmare of unworthiness and
depression
Today, I am living in freedom
Yesterday, I was bound in chains
But today, I found the key

So excuse me, if I can no longer live in yesterday
Because I spoke to God today... and He said, "I love you"
So today, keep your bigotry, prejudice, hatred and judgment
to yourself
For I am no longer your whipping boy of yesterday

Victoria's secret

I wanted to be beautiful
that's all I ever wanted
people told me I was
but I couldn't see it
so I put my fork down

Hiding my misery behind a fake smile
no one can hear my silent cry
the mirror never lies

they said I was starving myself
but they couldn't see
just another pound lost
and I'd finally be happy

but the joy remained hidden
as the mirror shoved the truth into my eyes
even though I was skinny
my mind saw fat and ugly

I just wanted to feel beautiful
but now
everyone is crying
at my funeral

Dear Michael,

I don't know what happened
not really sure
of anything
it's all a blur
never thought you would leave me here
under broken glass
where the itching never stops
but I held
with everything
and here we are again
one last chance to make things right
one last second before the red
light
one last wish to blow into dreams
the night
is drawing shadows with no remorse
cannibals hunt the sun down
making a fork in the gravel before every graveyard marker
do not fear my friend
hold onto my hand
I forgive you
I've missed you
I don't know what happened
not really sure of anything
except I need you
now
more than ever
the shards became tourniquets above my scabs
only you can make the bleeding stop
the pain
go away
only you
I'm begging you
to come back

and hold me
until my world stops
spinning
and my mind
begins clotting
carry me now
as I would carry you

Love,
   Michael

I beg to differ

building ladders from the neck bones of giraffes
the lions called themselves kings when the night settled in
losing their hearts to the jungle, instincts took over
they began killing other things
showing no hints of remorse
they were cutting the eyelids off
the tiny little bunnies

crocodile raindrops ran down the face of pride
placing a turtle shell over their hands of brutalization
they called it experimentation

the cubs were given the task
of counting the rabbit tear drops
the screams of the hare
could be felt with their quivering
shaking
their vocal chords chopped
they screamed

after ten million cries that never reached heaven's door
they finally found the cure
a shampoo safe enough for babies to use

Mother Goose

Little Jack Horner
lost his mind
Little Jack Horner
found a lunatic
staring
from inside the corner
of his mirror
He started talking to Pinocchio
making him tell lies
then climbed up his nose
like Jack and the Beanstalk
except this giant was more sadistic
armored in hospital white
taken to the castle of empty padded cells
following the track marks of the pied piper
into straight jacket shades
destined to humanities garbage fields
upon paths of forgetfulness
mirror less memories

Old Man Jack Horner
finally did find his mind
seconds before he died

He took all those nightmares
and placed them upon a spider

Sorry
Little Miss Muffet
Sorry for cursing your curds and way
sorry for leading you astray
into that alley
Watch out for that knife!

sorry
Little Miss Muffet
ain't karma a bitch

Humpty Dumpty sat on a wall of illusions
Humpty Dumpty made his own crown
Humpty Dumpty had an ungodly fall
Humpty Dumpty screwed them all
Humpty Dumpty deserved what he got
always remember that
and all the free men, women and children
took all the twisted pieces and buried them
666 inches deep

Jack and Jill
went up the hill
when nobody was watching
Jack went down
and broken Jill's crown
and nine months later
they found Jack
dead
with an umbilical cord wrapped around his pale dead neck

This little piggy went to the market
to buy some fresh pork sausage
and this little piggy bought some new sharp knives
This little piggy had an evil twisted mind
and this little piggy had none
and this little piggy cried, "Please don't eat me, not in my home"
and all the other piggy's cried "Wee Wee Wee give us some!"

Old Mother Hubbard
went to the cupboard
to hide more children's bones
she also kept their hair
after she gelded them like pears
left them in the cabinet with dead eye stares
and in the end
she named all the maggots after the children she ate

Bah Bah Black sheep
Have you any ammo?
Yes sir we sure do
a Winchester .357
then he placed 3 hollow points into the chamber
One for the master,
One for the dame,
And one for the little boy
Who lives down the lane

Rudolph
the bloody nosed ebola mutated deer
had a nuclear enriched tumor like nose
and in the transylvanian fog
when its fangs sank deeper still
you could swear that his eyes growled
and all the villagers
used to laugh
and call him names

Three Blind Mice
were all fed the same poisoned cheese
washed it all down with brainwashing juice
Now they stumble into the walls of reality
they do not see
outside their own roofed ceiling

Three Blind Mice
see how they walk
with a limp in this step
from Uncle Sam's twisting

Three Blind Mice
see how they run
peaceful demonstrators
being beaten and tear gassed
for standing what they believe is right

Three Branches of Power
see how they are so blind
statues of stained vision

three bloated pawns
floating upon the seas of unconsciousness
and everyone just watched
Justice being raped on the witness stand

paper rocks and broken scissors

I tried to fight them
tried to wake them
but nobody listened
so I joined them
and I'm trying not to remember
as I paint the yellow bricks
gold

I'm trying to forget
and do what I'm told
so I glue myself to the television set
the weather channel tells me it's raining
though I see the sun is shining
but I'm learning not to question
anything

Freedom isn't free and war solves everything
Yes Master
Somebody call the fashion police
the Cardashian sisters are wearing the same dress
thank god for the news at yahoo

The sandcastles are surrounded by moats of oil
but BP's flag
isn't flying half staff
Sorry...
got off the beaten path
I promise to do better
and not to remember
as I paint these yellow bricks
gold

The United States apologized on Friday
for an experiment conducted in the 1940s
in which U.S. government researchers
deliberately infected Guatemalan prisoners
women
and mental patients
with syphilis.
-Reuters

and all the gold bricks
turned yellow in my hands

pruning

they say money is the root of all evil
but it doesn't help
explain
why the children are leaving
disappearing
no one seems to care
that the faces of the innocent have fallen
from milk carton labels
and post office walls

the treasures upon earth rest inside the children's eye
but reality has become a horror movie
we've accepted the brutality
cruelty
pay our monthly cable bill

holding their ticket stubs into the air
the crowds cheered for Nancy Grace
while sitting on their fat asses
doing nothing
not much

like clipped birds
the people on earth walked in circles
while the pigs took their eggs
and tender young
for the better of all

The red turned into blood shot panic eyes
the white was soiled
and the blue of a flag
was left bleeding
in 1776

the people down below
heard the explosion
but never did see a plane
until they turned on the news, and had it explained

the homo sapiens were walking upright
walking in circles
when the pigs discovered a trip wire
a trick
that struck fear
piercing the avian heart
and with this one creation
this one
word
they learned to control
the world

Ladies and Gentlemen,
presenting... the greatest lie ever
nuclear
brought to you by
iran, russia, and north korea

meanwhile the mercury level is rising
as the ocean tide's climbing
they poison the food
then poison the minds with the daily news
the children are dying
and the old are barely
alive
everyone worried about nuclear war
while the whole world is going to hell

divided we fall

I remember after nine eleven
some of the reasons given
how the terrorists hated our freedom
so big brother came
and took it away

God bless America sang
while our liberties stood tall
in the arms of a giant statue

We needed to protect our liberty
so we allowed them to spy
"I'm not a criminal"
was the social theme
I don't care if they hear me
or see me
I have nothing to hide
and like all good children
we opened our mouths wide
and swallowed their medication

we loved freedom
so we took our friend
and water boarded them
tortured them
with cruelty
in hands that do not know
mercy

choking
screaming
crying
suffocating

biting
broken
bones
crunching
spines
loud noise
bright light
it was our right
so we tortured our enemies at Gitmo Bay
the media took america's morality pulse every day
with poll after poll
and teleprompter lies

the voices sounded human
but they had already been written
every scene was holographic clear
cut and edited
made to fit upon this screen
this machine

the bombs were going off in new york city
story after story
burning jet fuel
was the story

we got used to becoming prisoners...

some people began to see the little things
and they wanted to eat healthy
so the american psychiatry association
came up with a solution
'the healthy eating disorder'
yes, it's true
you're mentally ill

fruits and vegetables could not be used as medicine

ivory poachers

The Republicans came waving flags supporting life
but once you've been born
they don't give a crap
Just hurry up and die already
do it quietly please
don't rock the boat
or cause a fuss
What Would Jesus Do?
they don't give a fuck
they've already got the Christian vote

The Republicans said they won't allow any bills to pass
going to sit on the White House toilet for two years
wiping their ass
They don't give a shit about you or me
they've got the best healthcare already
free for their whole family

What... ?
They've got free healthcare
but how dare we
say it should be free
oh, the hypocrisy
oh, the insanity
The Congressmen seem to have forgotten
that it is we
who have given what they have gotten

They pledge allegiance with hand over heart
a bible in their back pocket
but the cross they wear around their neck
is Judas' kiss
undressed

take two of these and call me in the morning

No time to think
It's up
It's down
it's twisted all around
but there's hope
gas prices are falling down
$6.29 a gallon
WTF
I thought they said Pluto's a planet
What?
It's not?
How
when
why
Psychological warfare swayed the peoples attention
to the right and to the left
preaching from the podium of the TV set
sitting Indian style it became the living rooms altar
pay no attention to the war behind the curtain
but for your entertainment
tits and ass are PG rated
but the bleeding babies cry
can never be heard
metal boots crushing skull
bullet
riddled
wounds
too graphic "they" say

365 million dollars
was donated by US civilians this weekend
to end homelessness?
to stop world hunger?

No, try again
but can you imagine?
what the Afghans
Libyans
and Iraqi children are thinking?
While their world's on fire
Uncle Sam's children are watching The Hangover

No time to think
everything is upside down
we're fucked all around
soft news
bad news
"it could happen to you" coming this Thursday
on NBC

The most trusted name in news is speaking
from both sides of his mouth
Like a boxing match
they hit you high
then hit you low
right shots and wicked upper cuts
end of round One
Cue
the baby panda at the China zoo
sorry for this brief commercial interruption
for erectile dysfunction
Warning
may cause blindness
maybe mother was right
we shouldn't
talk to strangers
or is it, the other way around?

the machine

Electronic numbers commanding your attention
Electronic numbers telling you when to leave
Electronic green, time to go
Stop
Do not question
when you see Red

Stumble into coma out of sleep and into bed
Feed the body for eight-hour marathon
Swallowing the blue pill of artificial vitamin
A prisoner of 12 years propaganda
sin cosign tangent
Force fed nutrient deficiencies
Crack your brain, and serve it up matrix style
Runny sunny side up

ACT's and IQ tests
Personality quizzes
Grocery card
Book card
Credit card
IP home address
Know what you like

Know what you hate
Know what you love
Know what you fear

Walking on perpetual escalators
Always moving, always staying still
Hiding in open corners
Monitored stop lights
Tell you what to like

Tell you whom to fear
Tell you what to wear
Make you see what they want you to see

Learning how to raise your voice on paper
Petition with a click
Mesmerized mind-altering songs
Camouflaged grey matter; govt issued helmet
Repeating your number whenever required
The tattooed twin $nake$
Slithering nine-digit limbs
Cannot buy
Cannot sell

Another human turning robot
taking commands from the television set
Directed by the antenna
Produced by the remote
Put you to sleep in waking dream

A mirror reflection
A Live reflection
A Black and White reflection
Robot becoming beast

The image of the beast
The image of man gone wrong
Girls Gone Wild
Slap you in the face with JFK
dare you to make a sound
Tell you what they want you to know

Rewriting history
Revising the future

Nobody knows the pseudo authors
Illuminati, Council of Foreign Relations
Trilateral Commission, Free Masons
Vatican and Pope
Good cop bad cop
All the same badge

Puppet strings of Oliver Stone
Puppet strings held by three
Three kingdoms controlling the masses
The land of the media,
Middle earth
The One Ring
controlling the land
Photons from Mordor
speaking every language
Confusing the masses

Three major religions
All hoping for the world to end
Atheists seem the most sane
Screaming, "We don't' want the world to end!"
Questioning what kind of savior comes in destruction

Predicting gloom and doom
all predicting the end of times

Three signs of the times
The Crescent Star, the Star of David, the Star of Bethlehem
Sorcerers and prophets
False modern divinators
Forecasting self-fulfilled prophecies
They've all got their armor
Weapons and war names
faith that can blow up mountains

suicidal kamikaze swords
Following the letter of the law
Hansel and Gretel following the popcorn trail
3D fairy tails devoid of Cinderella endings
Lord Sauron forecasting CNN astrology
writing next month's news today
Archived until needed
Pump more fluoride into the water
more viruses needed
Big brother becomes a Dr.
Injecting his soldiers with no complaint
Surgeon General's warning, fine printed on every syringe

Governments
Religion
Race
One army under one

One ringleader to this mad circus
Juggling truth into upside down mirrors
elephant memories chained and tamed
Every ticket holder walking the tightrope of capitalism
only a broken net of communism below
Crowds trained to cheer whenever Democracy is shown
The animal trainers and caretakers
using brutal reverse psychology
Focusing on the primates
make them perform every trick
Look at the funny monkey
mimicking the finger straight back at you

Cages became experimental drugs egg
testing every poison
maybe give you the cure
desensitized, de-humanized
humans to beasts - animals to robots

Forced evolution, Modern times
Secret societies, Conspiracy theories
All becoming a muddy flood of circled confusion
Cut your eyelids off like a Johnson & Johnson test rabbit
Sorry, this one's not tearless
Watch them
as they watch you
watching your teardrops fall
They'll count them one by one
Collect them in a pan
Create a graph on CIA stationary
Measure the pain by imaginary polls
Spread it across the map of 101 channels of TV land
where the Red Pill is never FDA approved
and the artificial colors
sacrifice the light
upon the altars of our mind

staring at the sun

Russian spies
little white lies

once upon a time
innocent until proven guilty
today
that's just a theory

Russian spies
big white lies

open your eyes
the terrorists
are all around you

Tunics and Kurtas
dark hair and dark eyes
no longer
today
Levi's
red hair
and blue eyes

one day
your neighbor will be taken away
and the sad truth
everyone will look the other way

will anyone question
have we all accepted
the lies

fighting two wars
spending billions
in money
and lives
while the weapons of mass destruction
came from an oil company
in our own backyard?

makes no sense to fight the Taliban
when all the terrorists
came from Saudi Arabia
100 years from now
the ghost of bin laden will still be speaking
because they need us to believe
we have an invisible enemy
could be you
could be me

one day we may meet
in an undercover CIA penitentiary
water boarded
until we'll say anything
I'll accuse you
you'll accuse me

the fourth of July came
yet Independence day
never sounded so hollow

the patients are running the asylum

On nine eleven two thousand innocent people died
so Uncle Sam went to War
and killed three thousand more
Shock and Awe
everyone watched the fireworks explode
but no one in Baghdad was laughing
Dead children
wounded mothers
heartbroken fathers
Their screams
and pleas
filled the cutting room floor
before CNN received the distinguished award
for best editing of a War

Uncle Sam walked to the Middle East
began planting His feet
crushing the grapes and vine
He came with a shovel
started digging for oil
Black gold
Texas Tea

A bomb and a bullet
but no one calls it murder
The sheep of the Right Wing
fire their own bullets behind the pew
Jesus said to "Love your enemies"
but I guess
it's easier to kill someone if they're already going to hell

Love your enemies...
I wonder...

what the past may have been
if everyone
had sent Bin Laden a care package

On nine eleven two thousand died
so Uncle Sam went to War
and killed three thousand more

The following day, the patriot act came
wearing benedict arnold's clothes

I support publick educashion

sick
of teachers being called heroes
your title and occupation do not define you
everyone can think of at least one teacher
who was just a tyrant on a power trip
do not confuse a title or occupation
with a hero
fire fighters becoming arsonists
nurses having sex with comatose patients
giving hepatitis c and who knows what else
police brutality
treat every citizen as a criminal
lawyers and judges being paid off
foster parents starving foster children
and of course, teachers having sex with students
trust the government to teach our children
like I trust a heroin addict to use a clean needle
the department of education
intelligence suffering from constipation
Act like a diploma is your salvation
celebrate graduation
it's all an aberration
12 years of school
and need a calculator still
13 x 14, get out your calculator
had to stop at 12x12
got to know the capitals of the 50 states
forms of measurements
and the system of weights

give peace a chance

Sunsets blanketing lights rays
subliminal peripheral distraction
attention span a short fuse
Strangers teaching our children
even at Sunday school
where everyone is born a sinner
even though birthed not knowing
black or white
love and hate
words from song
right in wrong

Laws of nature soon crossed
herd elects their leaders
giving up their land
the owners becoming slaves

21st century terminator movie
Everyone gives thumbs up
where the character who plays the enemy
can also be your friend
back and forward again
Stalin's ghost haunting the UN

One hand shackled
other fights back
with black and white
Poetic attack

A two-edged sword
Prompting mind's fight
A gathering aura of beautiful light
assorted light bulbs turning the globe East to West

Chants of Peace
soon become a song
different voices
some strange noises
everyone playing the same drum

A ghostly band soon marching across the land
no leader needed
all in one harmony
singing and dancing
shouting and demanding
the army to stand down

Holding the banner
"Give PEACE a chance"
shot down by a Christian .22
praying for the end of the world
instead of praying for peace
mistaking shadows for bullseye

Bleeding in flight
an Olive beaked dove lands upon Jerusalem
sees all the vultures dressed in grey
pointing their machines
Painting the new wall red
with the blood from Palestinian children

Hobbling in flight
the wings of peace
land upon Islam's moon
only finding craters
from suicidal astronauts

Circling the world one last time
this bird of peace lets out a scream
covered in blood from self and beast

begins riding with thunder footed beats
The red horse of the apocalypse
marching with a different banner
"Should have given peace a chance"

The Rider
singing songs
from the Qur'an
Narrating
the Talmud
Writing a picture book
with scenes of Babylon
King James castle in the background
all upon a red scarlet beast

talking in my sleep

THEY said "Freedom isn't free"
subliminally
we saw
there must be war
in order to be free

but the first and last breath I draw
won't cost me a thing

The baby of 1984
was thrown out with the bath water
but its stain remained upon Uncle Sam's beard
the hourglass was spinning
every 24 hours
now
a word from our sponsor

Peace

The eagle had landed
over 13 stars
Democracy calculated the square root of 50
the rich and poor were divisions apart
growing in hues of red and blue

Fascism bought stock in the puppet business
then changed the elections to the Jim Henson show
the paper buried the masses in an ocean of debt
with its reign
inflation assassinated the American dream
the eyes of justice never complain of going blind
when rumors surface
of tongue and knives

The bird of freedom fossilized into driftwood
the pollution of dollar signs
poisoned the 4th July sky
Freedom's eggs were squashed
by Capitalisms foot
Oops

War became an option
as last resorts closed their beaches
heeding the hurricane
warning
shark

The cries of the innocent are made in China
roll over

The carnivores ate
like predators take
leaving the Challenger in its wake
The demons horn became alien eyes
dreaming of astronauts
they built their spaceships upon the sandcastles of
Nostradamus

Benjamin Franklin's kite crashed in the Middle East
but the key was cut up
in tiny religious rhetoric
and everyone was buying it
the doves hung on chains for good luck

Forced to watch in bewilderment
Reason
was shoved in time-out
made to wear a dunce cap

the law began to grow and sprout

before the lips of the jury could speak
the weed grew into a tree
and covered all logic
finally became a God
the people obeyed

The priests were hiding under public official's mask
no longer here to protect you
The lawyers came from the land of Cain
writing new commandments up on Capitol Hill
the badge drove chariots with flashing lights
assigned to the priesthood guard
The Pharaoh sentenced the servants to make bricks without
straw

Behind the entertainment screen
children were born in secret committees
passed the test
and became law
the light
our guiding way

Raise your hands if you want to live
Sorry
Fate carries 2/3 majority

The image of man gossiped secrets in underground tunnels
but their hidden mission
was to cause an abortion
expelled from mother earth
leaving her to mourn

The moon was first on the list
Cut
that's a wrap
"Neil, stop eating all the shrimp."

Jupiter's moon cried red circles from Saturn stealing her rings

They sent robots to Mars
sending back snapshots
postcards of their vacation in Arizona
They told the people
it's exploration
when in reality
they were escaping

Left Behind

THEY escaped into their pods
then dropped the bombs
Screaming in the microphone
pointing their finger
"LOOK! Over there!
The Messiah has just appeared!"
burning the last drops of oil as they fled

at the stroke of midnight
Father Time's daddy
fell down dead

when the tornado passes

The secret terrorist cells were under Sam's nose tapping the
telephones
lines of opinions were made under disguise poll after poll
tapping our brains
and capturing our sight
24 hours showing us a world
they needed us to believe

nothing is free

They needed the people
to place their faith into elected hands that shook
the charade danced
according to plan

The Matrix tentacles lured the red pill away
come a little closer
it would say

the numbers became codes for the human genome
nine digits branded themselves onto the hand and forehead

The Nazi soldiers marched into the SS office
then walked out with a newly born CIA baby
the child was cute
until the voice of a serial killer crept into its cry
leaving no fingerprints to find

The Newspapers were being written by the teleprompters
pay no attention to the man behind the curtain
or the richest men on earth

The directors were producing tomorrow's script

The wicked witch was found by the eagle's talon
but the monkeys grew and bound
their tribal leader bred in the desert of Afghanistan
they hid upon the branches of beautiful Russian spies

They tell their side of the story with lying conviction
Only
and the other side
is judged before tried

The Commercials came over the loudspeakers
sorry for this brief interruption
Gulf War Syndrome
Regular viewing will continue in a moment
"The Dow Jones is up"

The Tin man was rusty
guilt by association
The militia's shadow whispered Timothy McVeigh

'There's no place like home'
became a synonym
for 'the good old days'
but no one was tapping their feet

The scarecrow became frightened by the so-called aliens
and the tiniest of things made it claustrophobic
a horse without color
rode into the sunset of Troy
and washed his straw brain in chlorine

Everyone was walking in yellow brick circles
Except for Toto
They tried to give him a number
and a vaccine

but he refused
taking off the collar
and chain
licking his wounds clean

he walked away with the heart of a lion
began telling a story of Kansas
where everyone is free
it's not just a dream

buckle up

we live in a world
where the authorities can kick down your door
shoot you
many times
then walk away
wiping their guilt
upon the glass of coke they poured
just before walking out the front door
placing a bag of crack in the crack of your sofa
their fingerprints were imbedded
but the dust never settled

Yes, before you know it
the news will be there to tell you the story
side story
Wolfe Blitzer screaming "Fuck Fuck Fuck
I gotta go to this shitty town and tell this story?
What? no Starbucks? Fuck"
while the offending officer is temporarily relieved of duty
the sheep breathe a sigh of relief
but the shepherds know their sheep
Baaa
Baaa
they cry out
yes sir yes sir 3 bags full
while some petition and shout
but soon the night comes
and there are other things to talk about
like a tennis match or football game
the herd become bobble-heads
throw a bone this way and make it meaty
with sleight of hand
they'll take your attention away

throw a bone that way
looks like Lindsey is upset today

we live in a world
where the man who penetrated your beautiful daughter
is listed under subcategory B
1. Teacher
a. instructor
b. hero

We live in a world
where the masses have been hypnotized
thinking they are the ones in power
"Just wait 3 more years...
then we'll vote you out of office!"
Why wait?
That's my question

vote
raise your hand
I solemnly pledge to choose the lesser of two evils
pull the trigger

another question
why would anyone spend a fortune running for "PUBLIC"
office
that only pays politician minimum wage?
somebody do the math
you'll probably need a calculator
12 years of the finest education left us wondering
what 13 x 13 is...

WE live in a world

where nothing is real

We(US)a
removed the chosen leader of Iran...
put a dictator in his place
called him the shah
then wonder why those foreigners are so mad
wonder why they took those hostages for 444 days

We(US)a
trained the Taliban
they were our friends
when they took on the Russians
wonder if that's in any history lesson

We
They
create monsters
then they create the wars
pause for effect
let me check my Halliburton stock

photographs of Dick and Sadaam shaking hands
framed in blood and oil
sit upon my fireplace mantle
alongside the Reaper
reaping benefits from selling Hussein the technology and
weapons needed
to wipe out Iraq's enemies (Iran)
Uncle Sam shook both their hands
while reaping billions in weapon sales
and crematory urns
the only thing bought in the USA
that's not made in China
but probably painted with their lead paint

when I was a young lad
everything we bought was made in Taiwan
I guess uncle sam
straddled that free trading fence again

We live in a world
where everything is out of control
but nobody wants to make a stand
cause saving this country
just isn't worth a damn (going to jail)
even peaceful protestors are locked up
when they stray from their assigned seats
free to petition
as long as you have a license
does that make any sense?

they said
be careful what you wish for
can't we give peace a chance?
can't we stop raping the land
and oceans?

I had a vision last night
a beautiful eagle held two hemispheres in its claws
one wing was painted black
and it was washing the minds of those it held
the other wing was bitter white
and it glued the eyes of its prey shut
as they prayed openly
there was no middle ground between the two
as the blood of Abel
flooded
the white flags half mast

upon the pyramid They stood (stand)
atop the mess they built (you ain't seen nothing yet)
watching us all with their one eye (Big Brother)
waiting for us all to die (only the wealthy deserve to stay
healthy)
Rome wasn't built in a day

war
poverty
disease
starvation, make that four
they rode into Babylon and even the priests befriended them
and we worshipped the beast unwittingly
as it stole our money
then took our attention
away
sorry it's late
gotta watch the Cardashians...
car crash victims
it's always hard to look away
from the scene of an accident

unexpected hunger pains

The flavors were hiding beneath the scent

the descent began with the first step

the world became a desert
and the mirages
my memories

mother earth offered her bounty
but my spirit refused
the water became my fountain
across this journey of a mountain
I took faith and hope
out of the closet
I took hunger's cry
and put it in my back pocket
tapped my brain
and the flood gates released

the color blue became attached
to the apron of clouds my mother wore while baking cookies
chocolate chips brought laughter
but too often
the off button
pushed deeper into depression

I walked backwards
and hid my older self
from the child in the kitchen with my name
and we both felt the ovens
at the same time
our sighs grew cold with the waiting

I walked away
dragging an epiphany
glancing behind,
I saw some reasons in the shadow
and they birthed the answers at my feet

why I get the craving
for chocolate chip cookies
and can smell them baking
even in my sleep

Poker face

Hey Judas, my friend
lover
betrayer
brother
mirror
neighbor
enemy

the lining hung with 30 silver pieces
around your neck and gossip scented lips

Hey Pilate
my paranoid public official
don't worry about me
please be gentle
please put down your sword
my kingdom is not of this world

Dear Herod
let's remember this is a republic
not a democracy
you were elected
you don't have to listen

"Crucify him"

but I had been to the mountain top
40 days without food or water
my spirit was reaching for the peak
my flesh dragging its feet

an organ played the growl inside my belly
trying to lure me away from my own spirituality

wanting to drag me down to Sheol
anchored inside earth
far down below
but I conquered hunger and thirst
the weakness died
letting my spirit lead this climb
feeding off the bread sent from heaven
on this journey
I had taken no money with me
for peace is free
but I offered a part of my flesh
and sacrificed it upon the altar of truth

tempted to fall
tempted for fame and fortune
tempted
to end it all
my spirit arose and stood its ground

a forty day lesson in taxidermy
leaving my coat and broken parts on the wayside
my spirit did the walking
my heart
did the talking
dragging behind
a dead carcass of flesh and hide
leaving the horns behind

Born from above
the underworld's skin tried to suck me in
in lies and deceit
but atop the mountain top
I crucified the flesh
and beat my devils
once
again

programmable

My brainwaves started playing the songs I forgot to remember

my eyes began to open with every turn of the handle
but the chains of culture and religion tried to hold me back
Walk
Don't run
Stop

the windows
let the soul's wind in
every tick from the hand of time
revealed the lyrics meaning

The sun was sinking
but it was only a shadow falling

Home again
Like a butterfly, I drank the Lights nectar
memory's fountain
pulled down the clouds from heaven
the keys were fires flickering
dancing in the illusions of mirrors
and I ran in there
head first

5 days without bread
that was the street name that led me back

the current took me to the river
where all the trees laugh
and play
then write the truth on history's ring
and like an angel

I began to swing

my spirit ran out of cash
rose up and tried to rest
but the flesh continued feeding
the parking machine

so I closed my eyes and found
Jim Morrison's hand
and I broke on through to the other side
finding the truth
covered in lies

suddenly a serpent's tale from the underworld
dragged my feet down to Sheol
playing music I never heard before
I refused the water that was offered

the apples began dropping
as mother earth began shaking
chattering winter
as her children
burned the midnight oil

the train whistle blue
sky burning green
nothing surprised me here
in this
my waking dream

wake me up when it's over

greed filled its pockets with american lives
eagle skinned wallets
red
white faced emotions burned blue
instincts buried
under fluoride's side effects
smiles from sinners turned ivory
the pearls went into hiding
the rich were wiping
their asses with gold
and wine
controlling everything
their faces never showed upon the federal notes
or Forbe's 100 list
the kingdom trembled
as the earth was shaking
from mankind's raping
and taking

the bees rebelled
refusing to feed these cruel hearted beasts
they flew into the spider's mouth
weeping
"please eat me"

the birds were flying
away
losing courage
their songs became avian mumbled gasps

the angels folded their wings
and wept
as everyone slept

the green of earth turned empty
mines of envy
filled with coal and blood diamonds

satan took up quilting to pass the time
as there was nothing left for him to do
awaiting the decay

Eternity only exists when God is dreaming
so he sleeps another day

Kicking Cans

The flashing lights were red comets in my fallen eyes
the tale lied
under wet bed sheets and blood-soaked sleeves
walking these dead-end streets
where faeries are buried alive

the knives were gold and slippery
salty
they sung a song of sixpence
a pocket full of lies
four and twenty demons baked in the sky
in the distance
sirens
blaze a trail of shame and regret
but the fire
would soon be forgotten in fine print
and a little boy's wish
fell dead
beneath the moonlight cry
and the flashing lights
those
flashing
flashing
lights
those blinking eyes
fallen skies
a comet trail
to my burial
the path
to a forgotten funeral

The sirens Screamed thunder
but the shots rang out

a firework display of sparks
and grey matter
The war was on 32nd street
but no one paid attention
to the lonely man on the corner
wearing pride around his neck
written in black marker lacking magic
written with a hand

that held onto hope
until the bitter end

so now I walk these streets
over and over again
the faces of my past are empty
crumpled
beer cans
and the only lights
lie beyond the flashing nights
into the red
where the demons haunt the dead

It's a game

It's all a game

the questions bloom
inside the orchids vein
the riddle's answer
hides inside the bumble bee wing

peace was planted with democracy's knife
using the first born as fertilizer
they fed the beast more and more
Democracy was the broccoli other people never got a chance
to taste
and all we could do was wonder
as Uncle Sam shoved it down their throats

It's all a game dancing under the eyes of God
wishing He could create some puppet strings
and get people to do
what is right

the smoke signals came in the oceans tide
some were screaming
Run...
Hide

Scarlet's children marked the prophecies with dots
trying to figure it all out
the christian authors were growing rich before the final hours
they preached

the hypocrites were dressed in fat black pastorly robes
holding the voice of the seven thunders, behind bars
They made an image

forged in the fires of pagan religion
they preached against abortion
while they sacrificed their children
to the god of war
fire

the master builders
disguised their intent
with the face of our first president
It's all a game
watching it all unfold
as invisible hands advance another pawn

I want a refund

They said the truth was free
but there's a ten % admission fee

Armani bloated suits strut
white peacock feathers fluff
"father pastor
rabbi priest
tell us the mysteries
the ones you speak"
24-hour deceit

The false temples began putting up steeples

They said the truth was free
but there's a 10 percent admission fee

confess your sins before you crucify the Christ again

The priests were speaking Latin incantations
raping the choir boys beside the holy water fountains
Their evil cracked the innocent foundations
until 20 years later, when they remembered the crime again
screaming holy mother of God upon the witness stand

They told me that this was the house of God
but it didn't bare His name on the welcome mat
Thought the truth was free
how do I get back
my 10 percent admission fee

The hypocrites were wearing shepherds clothing
Driving Mercedes
coated in humble disguise

On Saturn's Eve
they wrote down long prayers with the darkest ink of
conviction
Every Sunday morning
the offering plate was passed around
3 gods were hungry
feeding them with green confetti
they promised a blessing
while they did the stealing
even from the hands of widows and children
whom the money was meant to be given to

I broke the tithing curse
learned the tribe of Levi couldn't own any land
so his other brothers helped support the priestly fam
not with gold or mammon
but with grain and rice

They said I was blind
but I saw

I saw it all

They said the truth was free
but there's a 10 percent admission fee
I remember a prophecy
something the Messiah said
about someone who would persecute His church
he would come in his own name
he would come
with signs and wonders
and then I remembered Saul
changed his name to Paul
how he was the one who started it all

I broke the carnal rule... I doubted the sacred book

They called it the Word of God
but that is a title reserved for Jesus
the good book is really like the garden of Eden

There is a monster in this book
who came with the voice of God
But it was the devil
throwing his voice behind an angel

he stones the adulterers
he stones the sabbath breakers
he stones the woman and children
even stomps the breath
from newborn babies

At least that is what "THEY' told me
What would Jesus do?

nice try...
good excuse
today we'd call them crazy
if they said God made us kill the babies over and over again
But there it is...
THEY SAID, "God said"
hate your enemies

Jesus said
love your enemy

I broke the carnal rule
I said not all of it's true

I picked the dandelions and daisies
God loves you
God hates you
You're going to heaven

sorry
You're going to hell
seems if eternal torture is true
then abortion isn't so bad
the women in the end
carry their cross of shame upon their backs
saving their children from the eternal flames of hell
better to never have been born
then to burn forevermore

They said Hell was for sinners
and I was one of them
they said Jesus died for my sins
but apparently
not all of them

They said they held the truth
but I looked closely
as the sand
in their dirty hands
became cold and empty
I want my money back
thought it was free
they never told me
they never told me

they would take 10 percent of me

Numbers

Surrounded by demon eyes
there was nowhere to hide
they chased me down
dragged me outside of town
my lips trembled
my hands shook
my will
was broken
this was the end

Just an hour ago
everything was beautiful
it was my birthday and so peaceful
all my friends and relatives had come over
there were smiles and plenty of food and laughter
singing and dancing
wishing and story telling
but once the party was over
the night drew quickly
and the cold northern winds began to blow mightily
my wife and little ones would suffer from the cold
so I did what any good father would do
I went out and gathered some firewood

but today is the sabbath
and working is against the law
so I had to sneak under cover of darkness
I risked it all

The first stone
was aimed at my head
I closed my eyes and braced myself
but it flew overhead

but then
the sky became black
as rocks rained down from the heavens

and the people cheered

I searched through the crowd
past their blood thirsty mouths
with blood pouring
my eyes thick with red
I begged for mercy
said I'd never do it again
said I was sorry
I did it for my family
but I saw their hearts
blacker than midnight
and harder than marble
I realized then
my world was done

they threw rocks at my face
shattered all my teeth
my tongue lay lifeless
beneath torn flesh and gum
my fingers
they are all broken
I can see the bones protruding through them
my toes and feet
lie in a pool of clotted agony
my legs shattered
on the ground I lay
with my arms covering my face
but
they never stopped
I could not see myself
but I must have been black and blue

some of my skin
lay beside me
and when the sharp stones
hit my exposed skin
my nerves raged on fire
I gurgled my own blood
and soon it became a fountain

I passed out
over and over
again and again

my family
my friends
just an hour ago
you loved me
but now
you've come to destroy me
you come with death
with God on your lips
and misery under your breath

I can't explain
there are no words for this excruciating pain
I just wanted you to know
that before I died
under the piles of jagged stone
I heard the voice of an angel
It was Loud
and it was Clear
I can't say it wasn't a hallucination
some of you may sneer
I won't tell you what He said
Just listen to my advice
Don't believe everything you read

if you want to know God
then close your books
and open your heart
that would be the first place
to start

Numbers 15
"Now while the children of Israel were in the wilderness, they
found a man gathering sticks on the Sabbath day. And those
who found him gathering sticks brought him to Moses and
Aaron, and to all the congregation. They put him under
guard, because it had not been explained what should be done
to him.
Then the LORD said to Moses, "The man must surely be put
to death; all the congregation shall stone him with stones
outside the camp." So, as the LORD commanded Moses, all
the congregation brought him outside the camp and stoned
him with stones, and he died."

Doctrines of Darkness...

Blinding the masses.
Trees of Corruption
Petrified in Stone...
Mother may I...
Flee from Egypt.

Mother may I
Escape from Sodom
Mother May I
Be free from Babylon

Life, Death and Resurrection
The 12th apostle is chosen
A great light and voice is heard
Dreams and Revelations

Mother may I...
Flee from Egypt.
Mother may I
Escape from Sodom
Mother May I
Be free from Babylon

Words of Truth Light and Spirit
Washed away in this flood of Darkness
Waves of Doctrines crash over and over
Some cling to Life, while others drift away

Mother may I... Flee from Egypt
Mother may I
Escape from Sodom
Mother May I... Be free from Babylon

The word of God chosen over the Voice of God
Reading without listening, the Spirit of Truth still speaks
Gluttons praying over meals, while greed passes the plate
Idols and images, steeples and crosses,
Judging the innocent, condemning the children
Doctrines of Darkness
Blinding the masses
Mother may I…
Flee from slavery.
Mother may I
Escape from this world
Mother May I
Be free from religion

May I?

The bankers were breaking the Old Testament laws
usury
accidentally on purpose without remorse
or repentance
but everything was okay, since they tithed every Sunday
their fingers remained free of interest
the middle stood tall

The offering plates couldn't be adjusted
greed's mouth rolled out the red carpet
speaking in tongues
it built an army
god of thunder
and fear

Bow down
and worship ME
even if you hate Me
I control everything
especially the room temperature

The cries of the innocent became tender red meat
the demons sniffed the air and tasted blood
so god turns up the heat
and lets them feed
not wanting to be bothered
by these
little
pesky things

Red roses never grow under Winters long sleeve
so we keep their memories warm and safe inside
place them upon the windowsill

in the sun next to mine
some promises only grow with tears

For ninety-nine dollars an hour, the lemons tasted sweet
but the water never turns to wine
except in a book

The story keeper died with all the secrets
hidden
Love came out from hiding beneath the sun
Its spirit dressed itself in flowers and flesh
and walked about
but the children of Earth
did not recognize her
so they killed her
and everything that went wrong
became a living circle

**thou shall beat him with the rod
and deliver his soul from hell**

The blind were leading the blind
and all the sheep
fell in line

The flock began to arm themselves
for war

the prince of peace
sat in the battle room
but nobody was listening

they forsook the truth
and worshipped a book

they gathered in circles
began sharpening their swords
blades of condemnation
they were too busy
to feed the poor

Judge not
Forgive
Love

those word were foreign upon their lips
as the thorns of religion
had turned their hearts to stone

the blind were leading the blind
and all the sheep
fell into a pit

a shepherd came and sheared their hide

revealing the true hypocrite
inside

but they were blind

so they covered their sins with the King James
their lips preaching hell and eternal flames

they said they knew Jesus
while acting like the devil
actions always speak louder
than mere words
they laughed at those in prison
mocked those who didn't agree
they stepped on the broken
impaled the suffering
rubbing salt
in their wounds

the blind were leading the blind
they said 'We See'
but they had become
the Pharisee

the world was going to hell
and they could not wait

the sound of war - brought them joy
starving children - gave them glee
every catastrophe
the oil in the sea
it all made them so happy
another prophecy, another sign
their king was coming
to take them home

The blind were leading the blind

locking the door to the kingdom behind
but soon the storm came
and all the stones they threw
buried them alive

and then the sun arose
the light that had been hidden
began shining from heaven
the key
once again given

Mercy

the blind hitch hiker

I move into the pain
standing in its silhouette
I push into the pain
until the endorphins scream my middle name

pushing past fatigue
exhaustion takes three deep breaths

embrace the agony
as muscle tissue tears like paper machete
passing thresholds
making new boundaries
retrieving musty memories

parts of my former self
are moving
away

drifting
further and further

but I have neither
the desire or strength
to retrieve them for namesake

let them be
as debris
floating into outer space
weightlessly
farther and farther
away

goodbye my former self

I will never miss you
good riddance

the air breathes clearer these days
the ground is softer today
my coated tongue of yesterday
gives way to licorice raspberry
twisting
free
lighter than before
higher than ever
before

the helium balloons released

I scan the horizon
in search for my soul mate
and in the forsaken distance
deja vu remains silent

riddles of your fainted scent
drift further
and further
away

will it ever remain
this dream

will it ever become still
catch able
reasonable
will I ever be able
or will it continue to drift
one more day away
further
further away

the sun never sets
today never comes
everything is always
moving
sifting
drifting
further and further away

my vocal chords take ownership of themselves and scream for
help
suddenly
all the planets are staring at me
and I wish I could
vanish
into the sea
of forgotten memories
where pain was only in fairy tales
and all the pumpkin patches
became car dealerships
when the clock strikes midnight
the witching hour
where the dead hide in their graves
their bodies wasting away
into nothingness

Across the desert

I saw a scarred Lion
walking away from jerusalem
carrying a cross
and a crown
crossing the desert of Babylon

upon his shoulders
he carried the world

he was seeking those who were lost and frozen
wanting to warm them
by the fire in his eyes
wanting to wrap them in blankets of love

He said what I give to you is free
and all that I ask of thee
is for you to do the same
to your fellow man

the desert became the hands of time
as the voice of wisdom
suddenly wept

Walking across the land
Every step
a leap of faith
as the mustard seed tree
had begun to disintegrate

the lion saw a couple of cubs
drawing up the wishing well
three times a day...
but to their dismay, their mouths were left empty

it approached the young cubs
holding a pitcher
between its paws
a water that never falls

but the cubs
turned out to be clubs
wrapped in leather and twisted mane

a parade passed
more of a mirage than an illusion
he tried to get their attention
but they never saw him
as their eyes had become invisible

weary
and teary
wanting to rest
the lion found a manger with his name on it
but once again
there was no room
at the inn

and so he walks
carrying a cross and a crown
walking the deserts of Babylon
seeking the meek
the hungry
and weak
wanting to speak

'Come here my child
rest in my arms
let me hold you
if only
for just a little while'

hypocrisy

A small seed is cast into the ground
Nourished with thoughts and reckoning
Darkened with waters of wrong intent
It breaks the ground with hypocrisy's sound

Spreads into vines it entangles and weaves
Tightening upon branches just now given life
Constricting its claws with pain inflicting
Look upon your heart, and see all the leaves

Nourished with pride and jealous doubt
Upward its consuming spiral
Strengthening roots in hearts decayed
The vine becomes a tree from once sprout

The flowers now bloom with hypocrisy's scent
Your minds now tormented into descent
Your face becomes ugly while you scream
Ego is fooled with prideful extreme

With lips on fire they diggeth up evil
Whispers of violence enticing your neighbors
Shutting eyes to evil while moving it to pass
Hand joined in hand, the prideful hearts stand

"Crucify him" screams hypocrisy
With brutal hand and prideful flesh
"Crucify him" the spirit screams
Blinded with eyes full of beams

Crucify him the spirit cries out
It's tongue lashing, gnashing
And threshing about

Crucify him, it's hypocrisy's voice

Hypocrisy speaks
She cries through the streets
Like the pied piper
The masses follow her to destruction

Escape her clutches
Into wisdom let us stand
With love all around us
Upon truth, not sinking sand

Stand upon the rock
When hypocrisy's flood comes
Anchor your heart upon the one who is love
Lest you be swept away into hypocrisy's flood

family reunion

the prodigal son was passed around
from infancy to ink
but the real story was buried with analogy
reading between metaphors and highlights
the colors of hindsight came into focus

the angels who had fallen down
were given a second chance around
paying their penance wearing bars of flesh
living without a halo
birthed into a prison sphere
born into a world of sorrow
and pain
eternity became tomorrow
distant from the father
they dwelt in a far country

forced into slavery
the manna from heaven
stopped raining
the earth's food refused to whet their appetite
stuck in the mire eating pig slop
some were wandering
some were seeking the truth
in a labyrinth of history

but in the midst of it all
a lion had come down
and paved the way
leaving bread and water
for the long journey

the angels that remained faithful
the elder brother
couldn't understand
why the father killed
the sacrificial lamb
then sent his beloved son down to Sheol
to reclaim the lost souls

the rebellion
was forgiven

and the father's love
came with blood
gift wrapped in mercy

the arch angel approached the throne
to utter a complaint
but the father would have none of it
Your brother was dead
Your sister was lost
but is found again

and the celebration began

the 7th trumpet was blown
for all of Heaven's children
were finally coming home

dead men bones

Religion
had taken the eyes of Jesus Christ
and painted them black
then played behind his back
pin the tail on the donkey

The star of bethlehem grew
to despise
the crescent moon
while the star of david
fanned the fuel

everyone was playing the name game
but only the atheists were chosen
to go to hell

so uncle sam started the chainsaw
and cut down the other trees
it's always easier to kill somebody
if their fate
is already sealed

the fanatics from islam were giving everybody
a bad taste
of what could be

the writing on the wall
was plain for all to see
that the rich were in control
and our vote didn't mean a thing

The homeless were growing
hungrier

while NASA grew drunk at the buffet table
Fuck the homeless
spoke the CNN poll
exploring
is far more important
just make more laws
to hide the unfortunate
for our hearts have grown hard
I don't want to see them

begging
or crying
not in my backyard
or within the church's wall

The 20th century cycled pass
with seasons of violence and war
the message in a bottle
lie broken upon the shore
under bridges burned
and Vatican walls
sinking with the promise of blue
falling in the night
the rise of the Mayan calendar
gave everyone a piece of insight

The light bled shadows colored red
while the hoof-beats dripped with every drop of rhyme
The wine was free
paid by Heaven's son
in gold, myrrh, and blood

Babel's tower was resurrected
but the sacred texts were only steps
leading nowhere

The closet doors opened
without need of a skeleton key
the spirits were finally breaking free
and in the end
long story short
flying free
I saw a new heaven
and a new earth come down
the past had been wiped clean
forgiven
and after six days of sweat and toil
humanity found peace on the sabbath
and mankind rested

bitter sweet

I ate the book given me
tasting the pages of history
democracy's knife slipped in the republic's hand
and freedom was lost in translation
Liberty sang
but her song sounded sad
and nobody listened
anymore

The machines were being run by wicked men
Big Brother paid off the pastors
monsters
vile incomprehensible
they read Revelation, drooling together

The number of the beast
was the snake hidden behind every social security number
no one could be employed
or hold a bank account
without it
The number was branded
into our memorization
The serpent with nine digits
poured from our lips
with ease

"Prisoner 666-12-2486
step forward
and take your medication"

The bearded fellow wearing the red white and blue hat
placed a bet
with the old man wearing a funny looking cap

but the dealer
was the true puppet master
and every joker had been removed from the deck
or assassinated
behind society's back

Behind the scenes
pulling the strings
they played a monster's HAARP
while the television set held the people's attention
ten thousand birds fell down dead
the audio was in stereo
but all the answers were mute
Exhibit A
a million fish rot in the sea
c. all the above

The sheep were faithful
all they needed
was a shepherd
for the night was coming
to sleep
melting reality
with futuristic dreams
and nightmares

Cyborgs of flesh
became aliens on their own planet
even the moon hid her shadow
and darkened her light
until it resembled a tattered white flag

Speaking in tongues
the master plan began to unfold
with every news broadcast

THEY
needed everyone to believe
the end of the world
was at hand

but even so
the wise men
and women
were still seeking
following the stars still shining
until the third eye began opening
a new story began writing
and the century closed its book
as the ending became a new
beginning
and the seventh trumpet blew

Fire and Ice

The ink was bleeding from everyone's fingers

the muse of joy cried with sadness
laughter began weeping
when the news broke out
Love, was missing

The Edgar Allen Ravens
had taken her to Babylon

but not many seemed to notice
as their hearts had slowly frozen

in the land of freedom
fear had taken hold
its grip, turned the eyes of the children
fear had rolled into the night
and with it
paranoia's fog and misty doubt

The guardians of the temple
were sent out to fight
the war
that never ended
leaving Love alone
unattended

left with her two only companions
hope and faith
they journeyed to the highest peak
looked down upon the world

All eyes froze with despair
hope, lost her footing
faith, began clinging to jagged rocks

Through the mist of doubt
the black skeletons crept
unleashing midnight's bird of prey

the weeds betrayed their queen
telling the enemy where she'd been

out of the sun they came

their winged talons sinking deep
Love was carried away...
to the carnival

the freak show
where greed cracks the whip
and the taste of lust never fulfills
where oil spills
chemical pollution top kill
"drill baby drill"
"yes we can"
deplete our world once again

apathy rules the day
and ignorance, the night

already set in motion
the butterfly-effect
churns the ocean

The seals peel themselves
as the dust is blown away by bullet shells
confusion is the religion of the day

in the land of the dark, and the grey
the blue herons are painted black
the ducks cannot sing or quack
their homes consumed
in petroleum soup

in the distance,
Hope screams to her children
Faith
began tearing the pages
but the power of hunger
left the children dry, deaf and mute

All that has been foretold
Raining down the rabbit hole

Thunder and lightning unleash the seven thunders
words hidden and unspoken by others

The climax is at hand
Wisdom unabated by man
A day late and so many dollars choke
The world stage a grand scheme of Risk mirrors smoke
Illusion puppet parade

Many blood sucking parasites have already been paid
The symbol the masses think is peace
Is laced in greed with the bloodline of 13
No longer carries Solomon's wisdom
These are the wicked seed of perdition
Even if I were to call them out
It is too late now
Easily in a day of fear
To label anyone a terrorist, even Love, my dear
Masking their disguise

Babylon system suicide

in the end
Love always stands for freedom
stands upon the solid ground
but now
Unable to reach or look down
Love has to look away
and has no place with those asleep
in zombie haze

when doves cry

China put a saddle on Sam Walton's back then cracked the
whip
the domino's began falling into place
the earth started to shake
but the architect just smiled
the chess game continued

the face of time lies in the river
but its reflection is never remembered
pages of past mistakes were torn and missing
and the world kept spinning
as history rewound itself

we tied the shoelaces of our enemies
in the eyes of dreamers, the doves cried white flags
but power and greed came with alluring temptation
their knees bled as the cannibal inside them fed
they were crawling
calling nuclear red
the easy button

the alarm was ringing in the New Year
but babies seldom survive the harsh winter

The eagle began soaring over the world
robotic wings of red white and blue
the drones perched themselves upon the fig tree
the star of David pointed to Jerusalem
the foolish thought themselves wise
as compassion became despised
instead of nests to protect the innocent
they built walls
to keep us in

there was no escaping
the landmines were hidden
and voted upon
good intentions buried under the fine print
'trust' could not be elected
just a word on paper

the pigs were ordering the chickens
to lay more eggs
freedom isn't free
they demanded a sacrifice
hard boiled
cracked
scrambled
shrapnel embedded horror

Abraham and Isaac began fighting over the knife
the future of Jacob's ladder hung in the balance
Israel stole the birthright then fled
and Esau grew red
running in circles for forty years
the day they feared was finally here

Then Jacob prayed,
"Save me, I pray,
from the hand of my brother Iran,
for I am afraid he will come and attack me,

And Israel lifted up his eyes,
and looked,
and, behold,
Esau came,
and with him four hundred men.

And Esau ran to meet him,
and embraced him,
and fell on his neck,
and kissed him:
and they wept.

and the lion laid down with the lamb

the awakening

Like animals they roamed
but their minds were not their own

like clay pots
they were filled
with bits and pieces of alphabet soup
left over lies and mounds of deceit
by age six
the young were caught by the hunter's net

The trails to heaven
were hidden
by camouflaged religion

Like zoo kept animals
the people thought they were free
never seeing
the true reality
behind wars and national debts
never seeing the noose around their neck
12 strands of pretending
graduating

the valedictorians were the best articulating
4 more steps to educations podium
left the student's piggy broke

Like a magician
the Sorcerers chanted a quilt to cover the world
blankets of make believe covered the public's eye

Every word was filtered before falling inside the human ear

Like animals they roamed
Like zoo kept animals they weren't allowed to see past the
fence

Like prisoners they obeyed their Masters command
subliminal messages from the tv set
where the infomercials contain more accurate information
than the dribble they cast

smoke rises from the only map
and once again I stumble and fall as I retrace my steps back
into Babylon and try to undo every thought
blindly covering my heart
a new day to start walking through pus and sinew
eating the moldy bread of regret and staining my teeth black
gnawing the brittle bones of day old hate...
gnawing my fingertips
until they are dead

it just hit me

The knife in my back, it finally hit me
I never needed you
I can die all by myself

With faith of mustard seed mountains
self-prophecy
self-world imploding
Armageddon approaching nearer
death and hell are right here
my kingdom of darkness

Note to self: pray for peace

The end of the world, put so narrowly
each of us living in our own little world
end of the day
end of your life, end of your world
worried about the end of times
wasting away your own time
wasting away in a world of turmoil
the future is always here
not always bright and clear

Houses of faith shaking
rattling
falling
earthquakes of pain breaking
shaking
shattering rain
floods of blackness blanket colored skies
scorched memories from moons of blood

right shoulder bleeding from angels committing suicide
left shoulder numb from anti-christ demon clawing deeper
into flesh and tendon
whispering accented confusion inside the mind of babel
the number of the beast
a branded shackled slave
a wounded beast
once king of the jungle, ensnared in never ending bubble

a shell of earth and sea
Screams of drowning echo when placed against auditory
an empty infection rotting off your fleshly hand

better to enter heaven
broken
empty
rotting
than to burn in hell
whole

waiting for a rapture while the kingdom of heaven is here

sweet dreams

Born in the backseat of a '68 Chevy
I thought the ride was free
until I hit puberty
and felt my favorite Uncle's hand
wrapped around my pee-pee

I found a job to pay the fee
but He
demanded the check
or else
I'd feel His big strong hands
wrapped around my neck

They said the education was free
but it costs
more than you think, to de-activate memory
12 years of revisionist history
left us all wondering
who shot JFK

The miles were measured in years
The drivers came and went
but they would never say
who killed our favorite son

I thought the driver was one of us
part of the family
until I felt the shock in Kennedy's eye
that's when I knew the ride was over
tried to leave
but all the doors were locked

Born in the backseat of a '68 Chevy
sitting on the hump
I'm trying to open the T-tops
and jump

Emergency

everyone wanted a cellphone
so they could call 911
just in case
became the daily scene
behind the glass
everybody guessing
what's coming next

The directors had read the end of King James' script
and were trying their best
to make it seem true
The dragons were speaking
with symbols
inside incorporated riddles
illusions of Revelation and sleight of hand
the magician's wand spoke in tongues

The Sun's hands bled stigmata
the Sabbath was broken
but the stones remained silent
and the laughter of lightning
was only a secret in the dark
for the living who could not see

Darwin's theory

evolution had finally taken hold
as mankind's spirit had grown cold

angels without wings wondered out loud
about a soon to be
extinct species
homo sapiens

a virus had spread among them
but the parasite wore human skin
smiling in the ugliest of sin

the priests warned us of them
but no one warned us
about them

the guardians of heaven perched themselves upon the
courthouse walls
lights flashing blue
sentenced the beasts to life
or death

Like an alien, they penetrated the clan
bore themselves into a host
blue eyes
black hair
six foot two
they went to school
they licked and drooled
short circuited
they became the killing machines
running on blood and oil
born without a soul

that was the question rumored

once upon a time
in a land far away
they say
they made a deal with the devil
exchanging their lives for riches and fame

but the horns of cruelty
and brutality grew
dripping blood into pools of no remorse
some were said to have kissed Satan himself
offering their children for power
and gain

Dear Abbey,
Who are these people that rape little children
then hack up their bodies and bury them
could a human being actually do that?
Is it possible?

from
lost amongst the crowd

Dear Lost...
I feel your frustration
but I do have an answer for you
No, these things are not human

we have a soul
they do not

I hope that answers your question

the Georgia guidestones

the scarecrow became my tour guide pointing towards
Georgia
but the bricks were buried in venom
and the fragrance of beauty was absent from its pollen

the factory was branding all the new toys off the assembly line
twenty digits and four limbs
nine-digit price tag buried within

the devil was hiding inside the eye of God
we trusted
worshipping below the pyramid

Uncle Sam died upon the toilet seat
they called it suicide
but it was the same bullet
that killed JFK's secret

the UN held the strings of fate
played it like a puppet upon the world stage
upon land, religion mounted a black stallion
said 'it was meant to be so'
and charged ahead
a monster arose out of the sea
calling itself the navy

the peace keepers are coming
but they're not what they seem

the sacrifice in Jerusalem couldn't save the future from its sin

the hands of justice grew heavier with sleep
nine tenths of the population

weighed in the balance
war, poverty, disease
these three were chosen
to exterminate the parasites
with an apocalypse

but during the commercial break
I untied the strings
giving the world some time to rethink
before peace and patience died
waving white flags

in through the out door

I put on the armor I bought on sale at the dollar general
ready for war
but the battle had already been won

the angels came down from heaven wearing sheets of glass to
hide their nakedness
falling between the raindrops
Lucifer painted greed the color of gold
then placed it at the end of every rainbow

the yellow brick road was straight and narrow
but you needed a magnifying glass to find the hidden path

I didn't want to be left behind so I played their lottery
then got struck by lightning
the shark's appetite grew legs
circling me in the shadow's vulture

the desert heat stood up from behind the mountain
commanding my attention
I bowed with thirsty lips

Every life is a universe
another world
between the shining stars and black holes
the moon becomes full of sunlight

The questions were answered by the constellations
but they can no longer speak of them
so their ghosts come down to take a peek
dancing upon the tombstones of those who have been set free
for the next breath after death
comes from a newborn baby

the finish line was invisible
you had to exit
to enter
the other side

the stairway to heaven
sometimes lies
behind yellow police tape
under white chalk lines

storm chasers

embrace the pain
embrace the rain

kiss the rain
then kiss the pain
goodbye

the pounding of rain reminds you of the pounding from life
you were drawn to the storms, for the thunder shelled your
cries
but always afraid the lightning would reflect the color of your
soul

you used to love the rain, for it hid your tears
but now it's time to dance in the rain
and forgive your fears

drown in the rain
drown in your pain
and dream once again

walk with your fear
take them to a place of light
watch them disappear
as shadows of flight

Jump into the abyss
just don't hold your breath
see how far you can dive
and still come back alive

releasing prisoners from hell's heart
then leaving the gates wide open

where guardians of love and courage never part

it's raining, it's pouring
the nightmares are snoring
free to breathe
playing in the pain
making it rain
riding the waves

the four seasons

yesterday may have been your last
did you make it last?
or wish it away?
not much here to say
you should already know
that you are going to die

life starts out in spring
ends in winter
enjoy summer and autumn
before your season is cancelled
today may be your last
make it last
don't wish it away
for this day
may be your last
and there is nothing you can do
lived a healthy life
while the minister of 95 says your last rites with piped breath

speak your last words, then live them
not a whisper of "I should have?
but a bellow of "I tried"
for that's all you can do in the end
live a life of no regrets
you can start today
break the chains
of impossible dreams
come back to reality
make your hopes come true
walking past the fortune teller drug dealers
hooked back on the past
swallowing pills of insane ecstasy

staying on the ground
amidst the war of earth's downtown
give them your mind
then watch it disappear
where artificial sweeteners bring natural tears
addicted to sugar
got to get your fix
say you love me
then show me
by smacking me across the face
the blood reminds me of our love
only free when I'm imprisoned
my own mother nature
pausing father time
growing older by the minute year
craving the sugar, a pain diabetic
rocking the boat while remaining still
not wanting attention, but drawing yourself
watercolor streams from dry eyes
oil painted screams from bitten lips

the earth is your canvas
but it's all upside down
praying to the god of sugar
to help see you through
a sweet tooth to agony
attracted to misery
fading mirror of self-reflections
blending together in shadowland
elixirs of toxins
soothing you
colored with chemicals
coating your mind and tongue
eating formaldehyde preserves
drinking Evians sewer water
craving artificial sugar

always brings natural tears
walking around with amputated dreams
hand still grasping
walking around with a siamese head
from voices evil twin

life
it's the war you didn't' enlist for
9 months of growing and changing
from the warm safety of darkness and quiet
to burning lights and shouts of confusion
hit... before you knew it
never see it coming
sometimes with blunt cramping hurt
other times like a sharp knife
didn't realize you were bleeding
until you looked to see
shock comes quickly
gasping in horror
as blood pumps and squirts upward
getting weaker
becoming nauseas
lying down
words whispered
sweating from the sun
you look up
and wonder
if the bleeding is ever done
giving up
may take years
the scar that bleeds the most
the one others cannot see
a wounded soldier
10 tours of duty

10 years of lying

upon the ground
bleeding under the sun
not courageous enough
to tie a tourniquet
on this
your last day

yesterday

the absence of shadow

Death's shadow
walked around my footsteps
dropping thirty silver pieces
I could hear its breath
the swinging scythe

The shadow of death
had left
the valley
The Grim Reaper had followed me here
covering the sun with his hand
seeking to chain my soul
to a past I had forgotten
an evil sense of humor enshrouds the greyest cloud
It's hard to breathe when death grasps your hand
its teeth upon your neck
drooling nervous sweat
the shadow of death had marked his map
covering me in a portrait of bullseye
framed in corpses of X

You cannot
out run the shadow
Death catches up to everyone
Say 'Cheese'

It's the light
that gives life to the shadows at night
a distorted reflection
In the light
reality births illusion's blur
the snowflakes purity
seeks refuge, in the shadow

in the valley of the shadow of death
there is no evil to fear
as long as you're looking directly at the Sun
the eyes of death
can only wish
watching the shadows disappear

the auction

Waterproof tear drops
as painted raindrops
upon oil canvassed heart
A withered cold Picasso piece of art

An old abandoned house with fire crisped edges
backgrounded in darkest forest shades of blue
broken windows, creaking door and over-grown hedges
Rumors of a hermit still living there
the scary home beyond the gravel road

Framed in wrinkled leather worm wood
signatured in fiery flames of black and red
auction it off to the highest bidder
Silence echoes through hollowed whispers

A former carpenter turned shepherd
finally decides to buy the piece
Pays with his own priceless blood
into the hands of the master artist
The terrain suddenly changes
Cold melted candles becoming torches of fire
crooked steps and spider filled hallways
Repaired by his own hands
dusted swept freshly painted living room
Outside flowers bloom with sweetest perfume

A goatly old man with bat wings
raises his hand so very high
but the offer has been withdrawn
There will be no more bidding
upon this piece

Overcome

You thought you buried me
thought I was dead
but here I am
standing at your feet

shoved me into the casket
then locked the door
silenced my screams
with your last shovel of dirt
I thought the pain would kill me
thought this heart had drained dry
but these wounds have healed
changing me to solid steel

I've risen from the grave
staring you face to face
screaming at your disgrace
my love no longer encased

with holy anger and silent sacrifice
I can no longer be hurt by you anymore
from light to darkness
then back from the dead

my dear evil twin
full of blackness and sin
did I forget to tell you
that the truth always wins

no longer covering my eyes
seeing straight through you
I'm standing right in front of you
hands around your neck

and now I am killing you
burying you
six feet under
my own two feet
Thought you buried me
thought I was dead
but here I am
risen again

I have overcome

hidden, but never lost

Watching
her shadow
Flickering shades in black
I taste her smile
bittersweet
a heart of gold
A hint of kindness
all covered in layers of extra dark sadness

Hidden behind audio vision
Eavesdropping, her quiet beauty speaking
her mind daydreaming
to be free
free to fly
upon the wings of dragons
breathing fires of passion
no fear of heights
no ashen afterbites
walking in circles
watching her dreams
go round about
then disappear

her tender hands warm the cold clouded souls
her essence, a healing touch
a smile that makes the birds sing
an aura of golden peace
spreads beyond her cheeks
but peeking just behind the twinkling star
is a small black hole
yearning to burn all the masks
she has ever worn
and wears

touching other peoples lives
but not daring to touch her own
she fled from her destiny
listening to broken records skip
'You can't miss what you've never had'
forgiving her enemies
but never able to forgive herself
Encouraging others
but cannot rise above herself
so she wears a mask
for whatever task
a bold face
for when bravery is needed
a godly face when quoting the book
a mask of not wanting
anyone to know
how afraid she is
how insecure she is
how much
of a little girl she is
always fearful the world may see in
look through
see through
this facade
a half-rehearsed charade

I sit
silently
watching
studying
high above the library and courthouse walls
gazing down
this little girl
in this crazy little world

She has hidden
thrust passion in the corner
and would have killed it
afraid to unleash it
afraid to see it
scared of this beast
she feels the impending doom
terrified she won't be able to control it
fearing the unknown
worried that this force
would put a falter in her cadence step
marching to the drum
of self-labeled tattoos
told over and over
that passion is a trickery of sin
so she nailed it
inside the attic wall
told over and over that passion is of the flesh
so she crucified it
buried it
suffocated it

roaming the earth
with hands tied behind her back
they told her that passion meant death
an ungodly spirit
a rotten piece of flesh
all the warmth is gone now
caged inside her isle
she eventually forgot
what life was all about
so she hides her plea
and shows the smile she wishes to feel
she buries the past
in shallow unmarked graves
Flashing fake smiles to those passing by

touching those she wanted reciprocation
visiting the graveyard every day
and wishing she could go back to that day
pushing down the ashes of passion further into the caves
strangling the lips of reason
trapped in the winter season

Flying down
close up view
I see her own hands
subduing her
tying her own hands
in strings of forget me knots
I search for her heart
but
part of her diary is hidden
book marked with graveyard marker
last page written left-handed
"Rest in Peace"
notes of 'Sweet dreams'
a farewell homage
to infant dreams
told over and over
how to be normal
gossip
rumor
secrets
whispered by fairy tooth wings
The cathedral bells ring out
'passion is of the devil
tis the leash to Jezebel
a spirit that cannot be controlled'
So she runs
away
from cathedral bells
but the part of her they took away

never came back
her hands give a marble touch
as she picks up
the mask of steel corpse
living on her island
all alone
she withers away
slowly
day by day
for passion was as the sun for her soul
denying herself the life
she was meant to run
parched for passion
it is as the water
the tiger in the kitten
the cool breeze on sunny days
the gust that flies the kite
holds the gull in mid flight
the snowflake that brings the earthquake
the snowball inside the avalanche

I touch her hair
She looks at me hard
and for three raindrops time
think she may see me
but I know she cannot

She waters her flowers
then waters her cat
little does she know
I am about to open the door
and water her soul
with all the damned up tears
she has silently held on to
never letting go
she closes her eyes

and I gently lay her down
never able to prepare for what comes next
lightly dusting off the mask of fakery
untie its strings
and cast it aside
then I gently dust off her true face
powdered white
tracing bitten lips
wanting to breathe into those lips
the breath of hope
the breath of wings
a breath that sings
barely breathing
but fully alive
with eyes half wide
her body
always room temperature

Reaching into her mind
into her heart
removing the lies
deceit
dragging the passion
out of the pit
bring it up to her very eyes
placing the light
back
into her eyes
her heart
her mind
her spirit
hands no longer tied
but flying free
above the trees of world expectations
above the clouds of biblical prophecies
eternal astronomical skies

passion
becoming the force
which brings every breath
passion
the distance between the finger and key
fingerprint and string
between breath and reed
passion
the driving force
behind caterpillar's voice
and butterfly songs
the driving force
separating day and nocturnal
heaven and hell
the spark in every fire

Into her ear
I softly spoke
Dear
You have always been free to fly
now
it is time
to spread your wings
finally realizing
that her prayers had already been answered
the passion she wanted
was just waiting to be resurrected
Passion
became the wind in her sails
and off she flew
She was free...
Free to be
the freedom to soar
the sun rose again from behind her soft foliage eyes
a smile thawed its way and glowed as the crescent moon
her black and white world became alive with color

she deeply inhales the fresh courageous air
her peripherals acute
her desire blossoming
her heart growing stronger
her drive burning brighter than lightning bolts from Zeus
an aura of majestic light began to encompass her
no longer afraid to walk through desert sand
stormy land
drought and quicksand
no longer afraid from fields of landmines

Finally jumped off the hamster wheel of prison life
escaping out of the rabbit cage
escaping from caring, what others thought about her
no longer bound with chains
or heavy expectations
but free
to fly

only one final temptation left

a few lines of intervention

burn the masks tonight
and let the fires of passion ignite
eternal white

follow the Light

dragons in the canyon

She stares at the golden rays and wispy grass but only finds
bewilderment
none of it makes any sense
what happened
and when did everything go so wrong
just frozen still gazing with stone eyes
trying to go back in time
trying to find the right memory
the missing piece
the forgotten door
her heart dragging behind her sleeve
sucker punched
knocked the wind out
toppled the courage
and blew the lights out
now
fear and doubt
this two-headed dragon
take their place
back on top of the totem pole
thought her prince charming had destroyed them
but
he only hid them
for such an occasion
as this

When angels are born

the leeches are feeding again
their fangs buried deep inside the grey
too weak to fight
too tired
I let them bite
my skin is crawling
as our song
begins playing
the acoustics echo
inside a porcelain heart
the curtains are drawn
and I dare not look
who's behind

the caverns are lined with your photographs
and as I remember
I see our hands
never touching
that's when the spiders come
weaving their venom into thread
silken strings of steel tourniquet
the future became encased in glue

so I let the leeches feed
just so I can see you
feel you
again

the ghosts of the past
read the love letters you sent
for a moment
I inhale your scent
breath you in

your ivory skin
your every sin
your lips
your eyes
became the amulet I wore around my heart

but these memories
only fill the bellies of these leeches
alone in my closet

with every skeleton I brought back to life
drinking every drop of regret

the after taste
so bitter
leaves my tongue
searching for blood

in the darkness
my diary becomes a sword
and in one exhale
I plunge the blade deeper
pluck off the leeches
make them my dinner

I suck out their blood
my memories they fed upon

swallowing the clotted mucous
I break the door loose

fear and doubt
retreat

found my pride
hiding in the corner

picked him up
and put him on my shoulder

with eyes empty of hindsight
I hold hands with courage
lighting my own torch from the hands of strength
I stand

the tears dropping from heaven
retreat back into the eyes of God
He looks down and says to me
Well done

and I become the sun
rising once more

fear of the dark

The nightmares came
with every drop of pain
and everything
I thought I became
just melted
in the pouring rain

the past grabbed my future by the tail
held it there
until it could no longer fight
the shadows smothered the light

I closed my eyes
but there it was
standing before me
every fear that haunted me

Paralyzed
Hypnotized
a deer in the head lights
every drop of courage froze
strength hid between the thorn and the rose
pride dribbling from my nose
the ghosts arose upon wings of evil
with talons and horns
fangs chattering

in the distance
I heard someone laughing

the creatures of black paused for just a second
as a still small voice parted the curtains
a voice from beyond

I heard the call

"Stand up and shout
just look about
stand up and see
everything you feared is about to flee

stand up and shout
stand up and fight
stand up and face the demons of the night

stand up and fight
stand up and scream
stand up
and tear the wings off of this dream

stand up and sing
stand up my king
stand up and slay this monstrous thing"

this song began to echo and ring
over and over again
and soon I began to sing
soon I began
to live again

I rose from the grave
and stood
between a shadow of a doubt
drew my sword
prepared for battle
sink or swim
live or die
I can no longer hide
now or never

I pulled the lever and opened my eyes
and to my surprise
the storm gave way to the most beautiful sunrise

Dear Diary...

Fear is not real

the wayside

I've got a full tank of gas
and a pocket full of lint
found some hope by the wayside
some called it roadkill
but it was still breathing

life is the highway
the deer must cross
to get to the Other side
but the cars of broken promises
tore it's hide
killing the trust inside

I've got a full tank of gas
and a pocket full of lint
found some hope by the wayside
some call roadkill
but it was still breathing
and soon
it's heart began beating

so I went off road
just to be alone
with my thoughts
making some rain of my own

I left the pain
on the side of the road
but someone picked it up
made a voodoo doll with all of my screams
but I was so numb
I never felt the needle's pain

The tank now half empty
hope began to stir in the backseat
I pulled over
and fell asleep

when I awoke
hope was in the driver's seat
singing this beautiful song
"Baby, you can sleep while I drive"

elevator music

Check in time
Storks behind
The counter
Lightly taps the bell...

The bell hop greets the hotels newly arrived guests
Wheels them to rooms of fresh linen cribs of lullaby's
Singing in harmony with little tiny hungry cries

From milk to cereal
Mice to rug rats
Scurrying around the indoor pool and breakfast stand
Where songs of Jack and Jill
Soon give way
To School House Rock
Playing around the elevator, wondering what it's all about

Teenagers now, standing under the measuring tape
Just tall enough to go on all the big scary rides
Always remembering that very first ride

The silver screens open wide
To a whole new world
Something never seen
Can't wait to get in - this love boat machine
Walking hand in hand
Wearing love on their sleeves
With candles lit upon napkins of silk
Two Bartle & James wine coolers sit
Party for two
A private valentine picnic set
Scents of puppy breath hover heavy in the air
Puppy love... romantic dove

In the corner, R.E.O. sings through the speaker's breeze
Buttons lighting, set to cloud nine

But sometimes, unexpectedly, the maids will often hear
The echoes through the tunneled halls
Of someone pounding upon double steeled doors
Frantically pushing the arrows down, down, down
Not quite fast enough now
Can't wait to get out
The doors an eternity shut
Inside, Maiden is screaming wasted years
Inside the box with one-way mirrors
Hanging by steel cables from the roof
Becoming your own personal changing booth
Exchanging long sleeves of Bolton and Kenny G
For ripped dark tank tops of Iron's Freddie

Dinner time eventually comes around again
And you find yourself hungry
Savoring the flavor now, more than before
Desert comes exactly as ordered
Creamy cool whip with lots of chocolate chips
Soon erasing the hurt, leaving shoulders unchipped
Trusting once again, you leave your doors unlocked

All the guests quite familiar now with the place
Strangers become friends, then strangers once again
And pretty soon, everyone wants to check out the other floors
And ride that elevator again once more

More courageous now, the guests start to explore
Tickets already purchased, free at the circus door
No maps are found in here
Not that many seem to care

Magicians and Illusionists

Buyer beware
Used car salesmen selling tonic
'It'll cure what ails ya'

Pied Pipers playing flutes to those wearing rose colored
glasses
While all the apes are teaching the high school biology classes
The Piper's notes soon twist into words
"Follow me, Follow me
But first things first.
Do you have any money?"

The women can be found traveling in their knit circle of
friends
A short clip of sex in the city and a bad episode of friends
Seems just like the real thing
With fake laughter from faking machines
Grown up girls on a European tour
Visiting all the boutiques, all right next door
Victoria labeled jammies, with painted toes and claws
DG button open, cleavage enhanced push up bras
Expressions hair sprayed, never out of place
Mouths covered in heavy lip plumper
Fake contact eyes, expensive eye liner
Window shopping - men shopping

The men of course, are acting like little boys
Trying to show off all their brand new toys
The gender from Mars, still hopping to bars
Still lost, not knowing what women really want
They meet at the gym
And play Madden 2020
Yes, all the males walk in circles
Still confused about these aliens from Venus
A dozen roses, a box of chocolates
All the while, thinking love is met

Hustler sticking out, from a worn back pocket

Too often than not
In this hotel universe
The planets collide
Soap opera's playing out, on the hotel plasma screen
Days of one-night stands
Their own private clubs
Soon hosting
Battle of the VD bands
Better just use your hands

The wrinkles come soon enough
And soon their paces slow
More like a painted turtle than a wild jack rabbit
In the lounge room now, listening to Tony Bennet
Everyone is old here, human antiques
Reminiscing of all those gyms and never seen boutiques

And above it all
Stands a stranger,
Not many seem to notice
Leaning against the top balcony rails
Just chillin
Relaxing
And taking some notes
With a grin upon his face
Gazing downward upon the never-ending rat race
'Poor little creatures, being swayed by so many scents of
cheddar'
He writes in his faded black notebook of paper
All the time, smiling down upon the circus below
While sipping a half empty glass of red merlot
But amidst the chaos and confusion here
Seems that death has the only one map
You can normally tell when his approach is near

When the clerks change from white to pitches of black
Becoming pall bearers pushing covered blank sheets
Down the mourning hallways, whisking away
Those whose time has expired
For even in the springtime with flowers blooming in May
Your parking spot can be taken, by the midnight draped valet
Check out time
Time to pay the reaper

Check in Time
Angels behind
The counter
Lightly taps the bell...

Your bills been paid
Rest now forever, in Heaven's grand hotel

wide awake

Life's foot pushed me down under
down to the depths of despair
choking for air
my eyes filled with saltwater daggers
my tears found a home
leaving me far behind
all alone
in utter darkness
the pressure threatening
I stared at the skeletons surrounding me
one dead hand holding an engraved key

"FIGHT"

so I scratched and clawed
Bit life in the big toe until its flesh tore
releasing me
I grabbed a shark by the tail
it had compassion for me
as my eyes had grown blacker than his

breaking the waters tension
I screamed bloody Mary
breathed the air I had fought for
floating upon an angry sea
seemed the world of water had something against me
up and down
my lungs filled with Davy Jones' dream
I screamed for God to save me
and that's when a boat began approaching

camouflaged in ghostly amphibian
it hopped like a frog upon the waves

riding the winds of three unclean spirits
arrayed in scarlet cosmic
the ship was named Babylon
adorned with stars and moon
the crescent moon
manned the torpedoes
the star of David
loaded the cannons
while the Star of Bethlehem
shot out dragon-breathing-fire
I searched the depths for wisdom
when an ancient sea turtle slowly rose from the depths of the
sea
It said "I too, want to get a closer look"

So we counted the sheep
two by two
every denomination
rowing
enslaved to the beat of the slave master
the turtle said,
"Some gave ten percent of everything they had for this ride"
I said, 'Why are they still tithing?
There is no tribe of Levi."
The turtle answered back
but the sound of the whipping crack
overtook his knowledge
and like an anchor
drug it to the bottom
but I think I caught a glimpse of silver
flashing
'they worship a book'
but maybe I misunderstood

just then we saw a lifeguard boat ghastly approaching
the sail was singing "we can save ourselves"

the people were screaming
"We don't want the world to end!"
and off they sped
chasing the hurricane

suddenly we came to an island
the blue became soot and soil
seaweed covered in oil
with masks of filthy rich black
the cannibals began eating
everything
until nothing

I looked to the sea turtle
with a tear in its eye
it had just died
and every ounce of wisdom
began to decay
and so here I lay
wondering if tomorrow will be here
when I awake

unknown

the truth was singing songs of zodiac rhymes
when my spirit fell in time
the gravity shrouded my feet

created by the light
my womb grew dark

place in a nest
Always out of place
out of focus
the shadows of truth
were carried by the four winds
bits and pieces
memories misplaced
the story was a jigsaw puzzle
with no flat ends

in the womb
the water was life
and in the darkness
secrets could be heard
but then the storm came
lightning struck the tree
and they named me

Time is a river
and my home
so far away
glued in gravity
I held onto every rock
trying to get back

born without wings
everything seemed misplaced
out of focus
I flattened the bits and pieces
placed the colors in their place
eternity's voice was still
the puzzle began coming together
the story came without words

the clues were everywhere
crossing the bridge of attention
I paid the toll bearer
in blood and sweat

a red robin came down and untied the nest in my hair
my mind became a ball
unwinding
layer by layer
cutting the string
I flew a kite
made with my heart

the questions were knocking on heaven's door
raindrops of faith fell beneath my feet

last night

Got my ticket
to the stationary carnival ride
Don't remember where I got this ticket
watching the world go round and round

riding the stationary merry go round
watching life go by, so very fast
stomach in knots, nausea in mouth

Wondering if I bought this ticket, and how much it cost
fortune teller can't predict how long it will last

sitting in the stationary roller coaster
watching the years go up and down
moving on the stationary carnival
where the pretzels are snakes, chocolate spider shakes
the cotton candy is piranha sandpaper
where drinks each cost, one drop of blood
Chasing troubles with shots of whiskey
World is spinning, upon this stationary ride
Still wondering if I found this ticket

Frozen, like a gargoyle perched on the courthouse wall
watching the people like ants marching down the hall
seeing with hawk and eagle eyes
always from a distance
crowded alone, in the nose-bleed section
step out of the traveling carnival
into the freak show
Where movies like The EXORCISM and MOTHER DEAREST
are only based on true stories
The place where angels and demons only exist in movie titles
Seems I'm holding the ticket to the red carpet and premiere

trapped in an aquarium of one-way glass
like a newt or frog on a tiny little rock
the escape ledge, too far out of reach
only existing, in life-sized pool of water
eyes and nose above drowning

Got a coupon for Denny's 24-hour breakfast
passed on the runny eggs and blood sausage
big bowl of lucky charmed aspirations
a moldy little island in the sea of buttermilk cream
where the natives are normal cannibals
eating their young and dry humping corpsed dreams

force fed with tubes down rebelling throat
finished the box, but no prize awaiting
reaching to the bottom
pulling out mouse-trapped fingertips

Got this ticket, so I waited in line
just like a clown
where you pay for me to drown
till my lungs fill with water and pop
the ticket, where you take what life gives you

From high chair to rocking chair
watching the world go round and round
holding on loosely to wild horses
watching them fade away
till all colors become grey
as you close your eyes once more
and watch the world pass away
Sitting on the back porch
Making last entrance into life's diary
Where every chapter begins with the same word
Regret

Dear Diary,

Last night I dreamt I had a dream
there was a dreamer in my dream
who looked a lot like me

Looking sorrowful and distraught
sprawled across the railroad tracks
all dressed in prison garb

It was my reflection, staring back at me
writing in his own journal and diary
with ashes ink and suicide pen
scribbling the same gibberish over and over again
each chapter titled with the F word

Fornication Under Consent of the King

Dear Diary,

Don't remember where I got this ticket
but it's time to buy a different one
time to get on my own ride
create my own colored sun
where the sky is sky green
and the grass is cloud blue
Think it's time to rip up this ticket
ridden these rides memento style, way too long
time to stop playing the blues,
and write my own love song

Don't know how I got that ticket
never know why I stepped onto them rides
ripped up that ticket long time ago

cast them like crematory ashes into the wind

God forbid, someone taped them up again
and gave them back to me

Last night I dreamt I had a dream
there was a dreamer in my dream
who looked a lot like me

Next Stop

Lost in a haze
lost in a daze
lost in this maze
saw a flash of light
but it was too late
my mistake
heard the train rolling
but I just waited
no trail of escaping
just a pair of cold iron tracks
flowing into rivers of black
shivering alone
arctic ice snowflake skin
I fell upon my knees
holding a knife of memories
frozen numb and unable to feel
I pressed the blade of suicide steel
deeply into my chest
blindly I cut, tugged and pulled
ripping out rotting flesh
chamber by chamber
removing a snowball
shaped like a heart
underneath the frost burnt crust
was something dark
placed it upon the altar of death
placed it upon the railroad tracks
wanting and wishing
to forget everything that is
and was

wanting it all to end
walked away
around and round
blindly following artificial crumbs of braille
heard the train whistle again
setting sail
I stood alone
anemic and pale

tripping over railroad tracks
I found the place I sacrificed my heart
expecting to find broken shards of coal
or shreds of shrapnel
I found instead a sparkling diamond gem
a heart shaped pendant
shining splinters of light
a glimmer of fire to frozen limbs
glacial lips begin trembling with hope
placed it into hollow cavity
but it kept falling out
so finally tied it around my neck

I hear a familiar voice
calling out to me
a ghostly spirit
approaching me
looking somewhat like myself
only happy
a halo of brilliant white
forming an aura
shedding light
through winter black
"I've been looking for you brother
seems we've been lost without each other
the Judas kiss
that sinned us in two

causing us to sever
has been healed
forever and ever
our reunion complete
It's time we took our seat
together
It's time to get back on the train brother"
Sudden realization struck hard
caught off guard
by my own spirit talking to me
forgotten memory
of falling off that train
into the abyss of stabbing pain
and almost going insane
almost forgot about that train

took my hand
brought a smile to my face
as mercy and grace found their way
upon my face

a loud whistle
a bright light
the train stops
screeching to a halt
the Door opens
as an old friend
picks me back up again

sitting down in peace
I realize I'm whole again
an announcement is spoken over the loud speaker
"Welcome Home Son"
and a forgotten memory is born once again

the God of the Beginning
is also the God of the End
and every new beginning
begins with an end

the shadow of man

the minutes were falling with the raindrops
but the pool was only a memory
a mirage photographed in time
only the wind
stills the raging sea
the mind races while the heart skips beat

gravity raised its eyebrow
wrinkled with threat

the trees begged for death
as mother earth wept
giving breath to a dying world
their roots were ground into fertilizer

the humans were hungry
some more than others
like little tiny leeches
they sucked the fuel that kept mother warm
using her blood to shed some light

all the animals lived in harmony
and they all knew
the killer instincts of man
the mammals grew small with fear

The cave dwellers fly without sight
the canines hear the bird lay her eggs
dolphins save their friends from being eaten alive
but the people have become aliens
eating their own kind

the king of the jungle became extinct
the last lion shared his secret
with the animal kingdom before his pride fell

how a baby monkey came out
the other primates tried to love it
but the child could not

the tribe had eaten a poisonous mushroom
and abortions did abound
but the ones that survived
were all born hairless

their smiles remained crooked
as their spine stood straight

plotting their revenge even then
10,000,000 years ago

Nature tried to fight back
but the power of genetics
intelligence
could not be undone

magical forest

the honeybees were stinging all the dragon's toes
so it lift off the earth, breathing fire from its nose
a bird covered in chocolate melted right before it
spray painting the dragon in a coat of delicious darkness
with eyes of blazing caramel it painted the sky
as it zigged and zagged - low and high
the villagers down below
starting screaming and shouting
as rumors
of alien abductions had been mounting

the baby rabbits were chewing assorted carrot flavored gum
as the dragon spun round and round
like a sparkling dragonfly sailing the winds tide
it hopped and jumped
trying to get the stingers out of its foot
but every time he touched them
they only drew deep

streaking through the sky backwards
some thought it was a meteor trail
perhaps a shooting star
so many made wishes from afar

the nights were filled with dragon screams
when something reflected
from the tear in its eye
a tiny spider
with a tiny spider voice
singing a tiny spider song
eight legs a week
a karaoke beetles song

"Little spider can you please help me
the toes are swollen again
from the stings of the honeybee
I'll trade you a dozen flies, some kind of beetle and the shawl
of a praying mantis
for just one of your leg giving stingers"
said the dragon with swollen feet

the spider replied, "the honeybee stingers
are the only food my babies can eat
that's the only way my children will have two extra feet...
could you imagine a spider with 6 legs?
now get over here and let me take those stingers out of your
toes"

once upon a time
an evil black widow magician
took the red upon her back and spun a wicked web
casting a spell upon the dragon
casting it to the ground
and extinguishing the fire it breathed underneath
twisted the beast into a fly
and that's why
the war
of the dragonflies and honeybees rages on
and the mystery behind the secret as to why spiders have
eight legs

Ya'll come bak nah ya hear

the plastic people were 100% organic
shopping with rotten apple carts
The produce section was watered with artificial coloring
buy two evils, get one good

over the loudspeaker the manager announced the special

the cost of prime rib was escalating
the tension mounted Fate's back and waited

the men were wearing black shades sharpening the blades
reaching into the cow's rectum they pulled out gold bouillon

the line to the meat aisle grew impatient
but body parts were half off
the butchers gave a show
flashing democracy's knife
another country torn in two
marinated with vinegar and gall

The paper and pens went missing
as the writers began living
the newspapers were selling themselves
The tabloids spoke of miracles
and pictures of hope were grossly mistaken

a theme song played over the radio
and everyone began to tap
and nod
to sleep

the people bought what they were sold
but didn't want to be told

where all the blood
comes from

They devoured the innocent
then donated clothing back to them
their hunger brought pain and misery to the unsuspecting

the price of oil began to skyrocket
as the butcher spoke up
"Would you like another soldier with that?"

bobbing for apples

the youth were advertising wrinkle eraser's
while the elderly wrote checks for their bladder control
medication
they couldn't help but soil themselves
as they watched the television set

2020 blinks in sync with the alarm clock

the sheep threw up their hands
then walked away
as the shepherds were stealing their lands
they watched the world through a telescopic lens
commercial free from the blood and carnage
the video games were being boycotted
as war marched by

teachers were handing out Rorschach tests
playing mind sex behind their desk
pop quiz
the killers were looking through policeman eyes

Uncle Sam took off his disguise
long enough to smell the poppies
his teeth drenched in blood
his body bathed in oil
the stars and stripes became dollar signs
and only the stock holders
cash in

the price of bullets rose with every victim
but that never stops a tyrant's breath
or tank in its tracks

the children were bleeding

crying

screaming

their flesh

burning

shivering

cold

one of them reached out his hand
with his last gasp
said,
"Take a picture of me
and show the world"

The Watering Hole

The turtles traded their shells for human skin
then casually passed by the road kill

their souls were elephants with wings
trapped within
a cage of flesh bound for decay

hearts were searching for love
while the mind looked for peace
but neither could be found inside the gravity

the map was upside down
written in Latin
religion came with testosterone's evolution
reading between the lines
the gender that bore life
was to blame
for everything

the apes were laughing as the turtles tried to run
some of them shaved off their back hair
then forced the weak to pick leaves

wearing pomegranate lipstick
the females instincts grew intuition
and neither could not hide any longer
they were called witches
burned with fire

the monkey tribe envied the lions pride
picking up stones
they killed those who played in their heads

The sun and moon
put their child between them
Love was looking for a companion
Peace cried out from heaven

the ants were marching
the bees worked harder
but through it all
the pachyderm held hands
under guise of giant tortoise shells
walking the paths they found to be true

new and improved ravings of a stark-naked mind

the crickets legs were violently ripped away as the violins
sucked on electricity's string
their black blood began bleeding
as the gold prospectors started panning
the animal's home was born behind metal instead of nature
bred to live an experiment inside the nests of steel wombs

the fat lady was singing to a phantom
the audience applauded with alternative laugh tracks
the lights were all on,
but the house bred contempt in darkness
oil and water don't mix

Pride and ego whet their appetite against the guillotine stone
the sea creatures were drowning in the salad dressing
the dead croutons were quickly filed away into never
happened land

the scientists were on drugs frying the children's breakfast
scrambled eggs
sunny side up
they discovered that infant brains
could charge a battery

the mercury was boiling
but everyone just rolled up their sleeves and took the vaccine

Finally
as mother earth gave up the ghost
Father Time committed suicide

the experts found
that the human soul
could light the world
ten-fold

and they called the new fuel
Armageddon

weeping willows

the willows were in mourning
the day the priests of the olive trees
gathered in the garden of Armageddon

the tallest redwood brought the priests of the olive trees
to speak to the elephant and the whale
the elephant came rather sailing, lazily upon an old giant sea
turtle
a thousand years old, ten feet wide with one lazy eye

'the monkeys have a grievance' ~ the elephant yelled

'so do the hypocrites' the blue whale bellowed

one of the priests fell off the branches
why must we always meet in the ocean, why not the forest

before anyone could reply
a great white shark said Hi...
dressed in a preacher's hat
he said, now give me 10%
of everything you've got

One of the priests spoke up
said, I give with my heart
and not by any law
he pulled out a coin
tossed it in the air

a monkey
flew out of the elephant's butt
captured the money
started speaking in tongues

"I can use this to make a memorial
to my great great grandfather
dear old charles darwin"

soon the monkeys could speak
formed an alter to the god of thunder

and all the hypocrites were eating yellow bibles

a glutton for punishment

Fuck this and fuck that
chew you up
then spit you out
you know you like it like that

They say all we have is Now
fuck that
now just came and went
without so much as a please or thank you
just a disease and a torn condom

they say the present is a gift
but mine didn't come gift wrapped
just a brown paper bag full of dog shit
the stork dropped in on my front porch
the lit it on fire before it knocked

fuck that and fuck this
fuck the world and fuck this mess

they tried to bury my intellect under 12 years of garbage cans
rotting my brain with state capitals and definition clutter
well, proposition this mother fucker

they said hell was for sinners
and I was one of them
they said Jesus died for my sins
but apparently not all of them

Yeah, they tried to steal my soul
with fear and control
they said this and they said that
but I heard the whispers behind my back

no weapon formed against you shall prosper
engraved in gold upon my mantle it sat
but that didn't stop the bullet from firing
or my recent heart attack

so fuck this and fuck that
cause the world is like that
make your dreams come true
be honest faithful and true
but the greed always buries their gold
just do what your told
just follow that golden carrot uncle sam dangles in front of
your nose
seems the american dream is illegal in all 50 states

so yeah
I ran their marathon
on the job training
but when I cried from thirst
they shoved me in the dirt

so fuck this and fuck that
Yeah, I'm sober
it's called AA motherfucker
so fuck this and fuck that
cause baby
you know the world likes it like that

all curses in this write, were written from professional stunt
muses
do not attempt this at home
no letters were harmed in this ink

the god called Law

The Law; feared by some, revered by others.
The Law; it has become an entity, a god to the masses.
The Law has life and power to those who obey and keep its rules and commandments and unwittingly bow to its directives and control. In essence, they are the good citizens of the state. The people have become the sheep, and the LAW is their Shepherd.

The police or law enforcement have no power in themselves, their source of strength is derived from the law. Without the Law, they have nothing to enforce. These are the Temple Guards.

The High Priests of the temple are now called Judges. Their seat is in the synagogue where they rule judgment in accordance with their god's written commandments and punish those who disobey the Law. These are labeled criminals or transgressors of the law; the sinners of the state.

The disciples of the Law are called Lawyers, and it is they who rule from the Legislative and Executive branches of government. They have written the law into their hearts and minds.

Just as a dumb beast follows its Masters commands, so also man has become as a brute beast, never challenging or questioning his god called Law.

The law has no wisdom, intellect, compassion or mercy.

Will you listen to the modern-day Pharisees who stand in the pulpits? They have committed adultery against God and have become as whores and prostitutes, for they recognized man's law equal and above Gods. The Sadducees proclaim, Jesus is the Christ, yet encourage you to follow Caesar, and always plea for your vote, for their next Caesar. He is their man, therefore making him 'your' man.

Article 1 of the US Constitution states, "Congress shall make no law respecting an establishment of religion, or prohibiting the free exercise thereof…"
There is no mention of a 'separation of church and state'
And yet, we have now come full circle… for the Constitution is only a man-made document and the masses have put it upon a pedestal and idolize it.
These are the Zealots, and like Judas they betray their Lord with a kiss; for their god is named Patriotism.

behind enemy lines

looking through blue eyes
looking through the eyes of the enemy
staring at the enemy
staring back at you

Reading through the eyes of the enemy
Speaking through the mouth
twisting the tongue of thy foe
filtering notes through nemesis canals

trapped inside the body of the enemy
its lungs, its breath, its blood, its pulse
yet you remain free from scars
only showing
upon the skin
of the enemy

Do you know your enemy
scrolling with the hands of the enemy

an angel living in a dinosaur
birth conceived upon death's bed
between thinly sliced layers of artificial bread
where freedom is the fantasy of robotic dreams

an amusement park of muses trapped behind glassed
museums

winter ice

The ice is getting cold my friend
won't you please hold my hand
squeeze me tight and let's both jump in
at the bottom we can learn to swim
won't you dance with me
will you sing with me
help me to forget this pain

I think you're worried about me
but please just hold me
and let the darkness invade our secrets

The ice is getting thin my friend
my world is spinning around again
up is down
and whatever happened
to all the sounds
my head still pounds
yet this heart is silent

the autumn colors have turned decay
everything once black and white
horoscopes written in scribbled shades of gray

The world is getting dark in sin
the light is fading deep within
and I can't escape
the evolving apes
are learning how to skate

I'm afraid the prisoners are running this asylum
somewhere between the good and the bad
mercy and justice both became sad

trading their clothes
for a pair of knives
trying their hand at cutting holes
into this ice called reality

Your voice is growing so distant
so hollow
on our hands and knees
maybe that is where we will find
that memory
the one you held so very high
the special one that made you cry
lost
upon the empty streets
of Christmas Eve

The ice is beginning to thaw my friend
and all the songs are static
the blue birds are all black sick
and with every new step
my tears cry out for help
It's all jumbled up inside
and now I've lost my only place
left to hide
so now I'm trusting you
to see me through

Your eyes are so blank
maybe you didn't hear me
your skin is bitter cold and icy
are you still with me
can you even hear me
anymore
the ice is getting thin my friend
So please
just hold me again

is there anybody out there
for down in the depths of darkness
there is a light
calling me
and now I need someone
anyone
to hold me
from jumping in
your heart has grown cold
my friend
afraid I'm jumping in again

goodbye
my only friend

you blew your kisses, like candles in the wind

sat on the railroad tracks
thought I saw a light at the end of the tunnel
but it was only me
walking in circles

seems I've found the place
where all my reincarnated souls are dropped
every turn out of sight
is another life moving on
a continuous lantern moving
some lights were shining hope
others a shadow of glory
some lights shared joy and sorrow
the paths never touching
rounding the circles
baby steps giving way to arthritic feet
sometimes the lights went out
without a sound
sometimes a scream or shout
from a sword to the head
perhaps a noose or guillotine
sometimes slowly the disease would spread
leaving a flickering light dimming and dimming
painfully going out
some lights seemed to jump and others were limping
and if you listened hard enough
you'd hear every emotional laughter
giggles from jokes
and soft touches from a lover's stroke
a splash and a puddle
from tears of faith and subtle
pain
happiness

sometimes they could join forces
several lights seemed to shine brighter
if you paid attention to the eternal parade
some were boys and some were girls
some were lovers
and some were thieves
one marches like a medieval soldier
with sword and shield in hand
another time I was a king
a former prince
crowning his princess, Queen
another soul remembers living in heaven
with God
and trying to remember
where His Family went to
All alone now
In a place of epic darkness
back before myths and legends
He finally rose above the grief
and found the power
to create a new world and family
another soul lives in Egypt
when the pyramids were the homes of the gods
and wisdom was surrounded by fools
another soul rounds the corner
and is born in the time of Eden
and remembering how Adam was a pretty cool dude
another is sailing the seven seas
and writing
because sometimes the water is desert dry
and the 'bottom of the ocean'
is really just a desert covered in water
the fish flying as birds
just another step around the corner
just waiting on God the author
to finish the final chapter

chaotic autumn sleeves

Climbing aboard the next seconds dream
I set my sails upon the eastern winds of change
throwing in some fantasy and fiction into my autobiography
hoisting anchors weight, the breeze of yesterday's past fills the
bitter blue skies

the thunderstorms greet me, and some even bow at my feet
out of the whirlpool and hurricane - out of the destruction and
decay
lies the dragon of hate
with armor plates of odd numbers and odd colors
lying in wait
to wreak its carnage and brutal destruction
wounded fate
the enemy of destiny
hiding behind the baits that caress the ego's hair

unrolling, un-scrolling, turning the wheel
setting a course for sunken treasure
a buried chest
of forgotten strength and courage
my chest branded with an X

Bound to the land of Peace
I gaze into a former witch's crystal ball
where even now all the villagers and former prisoners
are standing on the shore
cheering me on
trusting their captain to lead them to safety
free from earth's captivity

when suddenly
a stowaway
with a black-eyed patch
casts a harpoon
then a net
over a flock of flying fish
the ship rattles and shakes
as water pours from the cannon holes
leaving gravity and sea
flying up into the sky
away from the monsters of disease
but envy and jealousy took their place among the crew
and I knew what I had to do
Cut myself free from that society
flying higher invisible helium balloons
a wicker basket painted dream yellow
flying high over the mountains and valleys
filled with monkeys and natives
soaring rhinos and unicorned hippos

finally landing back upon my own boat
becoming the only stranger there
filled with bare floors
and barely a memory
wondering where they all went to
another storm comes into view
the sun peeks through
and into the rainbow I flew
the place where every wish coming true
eventually lead to nightmares never conceived coming true

a baby angel sings lullabies to God Almighty whenever He is
sleeping
the sweetest most tender voice that could ever be
into the reds and shades of blue
the vampire bats fly through

the fires of truth becoming melting drops of gold bouillon
turtle green children
climb the trees
collecting them with butterfly nets
putting them all into giant glass jars
becoming forsaken dead fireflies
writing last suicide notes
Breaking diaries of clay and stone
erasing my past museums
writing a new history
in French calligraphy
on freshly tattooed skin
baby smooth of new beginnings
shedding skins of hindrances
into a newness of future time capsules
written by myself from 3 seconds in
running past the 2nd hand cuckoo

time for the chimney sweepers to start sweeping
the fireplace in the heart of knowledge
in the deepest places behind wisdoms throne
into the deepest ashes of burnt bridges and rusty nails
all the mistakes made by perfections hand, falling away into
sawdust and glue

the hands robed in darkness
follow me and reach out to pull me
back into the quicksand and chapel maze
following the pied piper of religious song
trying to make me ingest their poison
trying to make me enlist in their war
trying to make me become the monsters I escaped from
so many visions ago
sitting under the weeping willow
just before the first flake of snow
fell

statues

I heard a dead man talking in his sleep
could I be dreaming?
my pale arms bruising...
he was standing right in front of me
staring somewhere off in the distance
he turned to look
as I turned away
mockingly
he followed me
breathing
heavily
soon the room was foggy
reality
patiently waiting
I must be dreaming
my bleeding arms dripping
perfectly
in unison with the grandfather clock

the taste of disdain echoed from cracked silent lips
his countenance grew fierce with disgust
calling my name from a voice risen from the grave
that's when his eyes became arms reaching into my very soul
he knew every maze
every tunnel
climbed over every wall
painting them black with every footstep
locking the doors behind
trapped alone
with the madness
solitary confinement

I heard a dead man laughing
thought I was dreaming
if only
I had broken the bathroom mirror
I wouldn't be standing here
staring
talking in my sleep

death, on piano

Death takes a Silent Bow
Crouches at the Piano

Icy Sticks of Onyx
Overshadow
Ivory Keys of Tombstone

Waiting, Waiting, Waiting

Dragon Scaled Claws tip the Reaper's Jar

The Coin Strikes Glass
The Chords Strike Midnight

Flash of Light
Sonic Boom
Clouds of Smoke
Shrapnel Shooting
Fires Raging
Twisted Metal
Limbs Flailing
Organs Failing
Bodies Falling
As Autumn Leaves

Tears and Blood Scattered
Families and Spirits Shattered

The Desert Sand Burns Red

Hearts Melting
Souls Writhing
Politicians Babbling

Tokens Fall like Rain
as Death keeps Playing
Broken Keys
Broken Lives
Again and again
Over and over
Again and again
Over and over
Again and again

Memories Whisper Through the Mist of Pain

Within the darkness, beyond the shadows of thought
It lies in wait, hungry, ready to feed
Lurking amidst fear and hatred, it cultivates
The harvest is bountiful - pain
Overwhelming the sense, it assumes control
The taste of death is imminent
Eager anticipation quickens its pace
Pride and lust fulfill its quest
The prey enticed
Web entangled
Woven in deceit
A web of darkness has been spun over my eyes
Strangles my breath and chokes out my cries
The predator smiles and opens the door
Death enters

Snowflakes Fall Upon the Painted Frozen Desert

The hoof beats of time splash through the sky
The silence screams forbidden thoughts of you
Freeze-framed memories whisper goodbye
Recollections denied, mentally destroyed
Emotions paint this portrait with reds and blue
Darkened clouds eclipse the horizon
The rain descends from my tearless eye
While the thunder hides my one last cry
The pain has been resurrected once again

This fortress, once protected by my guardian of fear
Has been invaded, the war will now begin
I observe from afar, and listen to hear
As the walls crash down and expose my sin
The sin of denial that has blackened my heart
Entangles my mind and rips it apart
Its fingers reach in and consume my soul
Nothing has been left but one black hole
The light is extinguished
My prison is dark

The Scent of Remembrance Floats Through the Air

Illusions twist nightmares into dreams of despair
Psychotic streamed visions I dare not share
It began with the emptiness of a farewell kiss
Plunging me deeper within the silent abyss
Within the darkness beyond the crimson sky
Crouches the fear of believing a lie
Straight-Jacket memories are all I can feel
Never sure if this illusion is real
Yearning for truth and searching for light
I mount upon wings of endless flight
Fade to black as this journey begins
The search for Christ who will forgive my sins

a mile in my shoes

Can't breathe
Can't breathe
Can't breathe
Can't escape
Imprisoned by fear
Trapped in here
Nowhere to turn
Nowhere to run
No one to hear me
A dead heart racing
panic tearing
See the pain is nearing
the dark shadow approaching
Hearing the keys jangle
placed into the hole
The sound of the turning latch
making my skin crawl
The door creaks open
A misery of light slithers in
Shuffling feet drawing within

Hoping for my knight
Wishing for my hero
Praying for a savior
to gracefully
Carry me
Rescue me
Save me
from this hell

The footsteps frighteningly closer
Danger bells ringing
Screaming inside

And just as the thunder follows the rain
again and again
I hear the familiar belt unbuckling
Again
Zipper pulled down as so many times before
Hearing the sadistic pants dropping
The breath of carrion suffocating
Brittle nails lifting my coffin black dress
A dreadful hiss
His claws spreading my trembling knees
With clenched teeth and clenched shackled fists
I begin to count the depths of blackness behind clenched lids
When the demon's tail
begins to flail

Drops of moldy sweat dripping upon my tears
Can't look into the goblin's eyes
The black ceiling, my trapped skies
The bride
in Frankenstein's laboratory
Past this horror face
is where I must see
when the monster is inside of me

There, hanging from this basement sky
the incandescence hovers
A flickering light
A strobing light
swaying slightly back and forth
it's become my self-hypnosis
My pendulum from oblivion
Look at it
Look at it
Look at it
Become one with it
Stay focused upon it

Don't turn your head from it
Rocking to and fro
I'm soon lost in it
fading with it
The devil's voice fading away
drifting further and further away
Fleeing from this madness
Broken sadness
Now retreating to my secret place
upon my mind's hands and knees
to the deepest depths of my very core
It's coming
It's coming
I can see it
I'm here

Somewhere in the middle of the sea
a place I've always dreamed to be
The sounds of the ocean become amazingly clear
Looking upon myself
from a third persons view
I am full of beautiful
Exchanging chains for bracelets of gold
Unwashed hair for a crown of jewels
Black dress for a wedding dress
Transformed into a princess
Sailing upon the rough seas
Looking up at the gulls
gliding through the sky
as fish swimming through unseen waters
As string less kites in bluest of skies
they begin to fly all around me
Smiling at me
Waving at me
Until suddenly, it looks like rain
and their songs become my screams

Shaken from this unforeseen event
I stand gazing at the ground
all around
the sharks surrounding me
each bearing an eerie familiar face
their black eyes becoming the soulless eyes
that stalk me through the night
The wicked eyes, piercing my soul
even now, if I dared to open them

Deeper still I must go
To flee this torture
Must disappear to another world
Please god help me

Galloping upon unicorns of glass
over the river and through the grass
Into enchanted meadows and fields
where four leaf clovers whisper my name
and butterflies cluster to my lips
sharing their nectar softly with a kiss
Into the forest of dreams
where fairies and bumble bees come to greet me
The hummingbirds dance around turtles with wings
Crickets and grasshoppers strumming their violin legs
natures music being played
The lions purr as kittens
while their kittens chase the zebra fish through the rivers sky
Into a clearing we ride
into circles of rainbows we stride
Where the tiny little leprechauns are all playing in their gold
red haired children frolicking without their hats
Grabbing fistfuls of gold
and casting them joyfully into the sky
I stare upon this wishful lie

When abruptly, each coin turns into the lifeless eyes of my
captor
even here, still a prisoner

Deeper now
Deeper
Deeper
Got to dig deeper
As far as I can go
Far away, escape this insanity
Nightmare brutality
the demon lies atop my body

Into utter darkness now
My lids are the window shades of this empty house
There are no lights here
No flickering candle
Only deeper depths of blackness
Past midnight black
Deeper back
into the vortex of silence
A place I do not feel
A place where I do not exist
a place of Nothingness
Numbness
Emptiness

Until the storm has reached its climax
Feel the lightning strike my womb
Awaking me out of skeleton's sleep
the center of my soul
on fire
Burning from the acid injected
Whip lashed back into reality
The zipper zips
The belt buckles

The demons tail hidden
Open swollen eyes and look at my children

The pendulum stops
The door lock latched

Feeling his sewer water screaming down my thighs
Crying inside
Vomiting inside
Dying inside
Paralyzed

Becoming the beaten dog I'd wept for so very long ago
A lost memory now my reality
How long has it been...?
since that first day
drug by the hair
drug in my body
drug through the mud
drug to this chamber

Broke and beaten
no longer human
humans hope
people laugh
and sometimes dance

Just a dog in heat
obeying the commands of this heartless master
This monster I once called father

Learned new tricks rather quickly
Hoarse screams rewarded with filthy rags of turpentine
stuffed down my throat
any struggle met with sharp blows to the skull

Resistance brought strangulation
but death would not find me
Even the grim reaper forsaken me

Learned to play dead
as raggedy Ann caught in the jaws of a rabid pit bull
The more I fought, the more I was beaten
hoping this primal scream would bring the final blow
But never so
My heart an empty hole
ripped, shredded, and torn
And then, my first child was born

Upon this hospital bed I now lay
Not feeling safe
Not feeling sound
Still broken
Shattered
Soon free to go
Permanently scarred
Damaged beyond repair
Blankly staring at my surroundings
Through the catheters and IV fluids
Through the hanging sheets I hear them whisper
Post traumatic stress disorder

Station locked on TBN
TV goes static
simultaneously
as I break the remote control in my hand
Last thing heard, a preacher raging about hell
an angry voice
telling me
where I'm going to spend eternity

Walk a mile in my shoes I thought, between the images of flying coins staring at me with assassin eyes; and the place, where my predators face, is traced upon heads of frenzied sharks, where demons play harps upon the blood clotted clouds inside my oblivioned mind

The sun never rises here
All the rivers run dry
My autobiography,
The next Steven King novel
Never free
Nightmares never forgotten
My body no longer a prisoner
But my mind remains chained
And in the silence
My heart still screams

hell...?
Walk a mile in my shoes
I'm still there

For Elisabeth Fritzl

You wore your sins like a silk necklace
the scorpion was your pendant
over your black widow heart

tourniquet
ring
you tore the curtains of my dreams

Misery loves company

A young woman stands in the sunlight, but she cannot feel it, for a shadow soon eclipses the light
She looks off into the distance… while a tear slowly falls from her eye, making a silent stream ending at her heart.

'You're worthless' a voice whispers

'I know Izzy' the woman replies back.

 Cold hands soon cover her eyes… and suddenly everything is black

The birds sing, the crickets chirp, and the butterflies dance… but she can no longer see them nor can she hear them

Somewhere, over time, this woman has forgotten her true name. She no longer remembered who she was. She has been listening to Izzy for so long now, that she no longer follows her own heart. Nor does she trust it.

She has become weak, and lost… and so she turns and retreats backwards into the darkness of the cave she dwells in. But she is never alone, for Izzy always remains, chained at her side.

Now, off in the distance, an angel has been watching…

The angel has tried speaking, even shouting… but she can't seem to hear him, nor see him. And as she retreated into the back of her mind… the angel had no choice but to follow. dimming his light now, he began searching through the tunnels of her mind. It was dark… with mirrors and pictures lining the walls.

In one picture, she was standing in front of a mirror weeping.

In one picture, she appeared to be very short.

In another, she appeared disfigured.

A black and white photo, a still image of her staring off into space, feeling so alone and scared.

Very distorted photographs lining each wall, each telling a tale... each a photo of how she saw herself.

And soon she disappeared altogether, as her emptiness and hollowness soon gave way to Misery... becoming like a ghost, as Misery now supersedes her... until finally, Misery assumed the self-portrait.

The angel quietly walks forward, and begins looking into the mirrors lining the walls... reflections of memories once past...

Gazing into one of these mirrors... the angel saw a young girl begin teased at school.

Another mirror... and he saw the abuse, from parents who were supposed to love her and protect her.

Another mirror... another broken heart

Another mirror, and she was starving herself.

Another mirror... and a young woman still starving for her father's attention and seeking her mother's love.

Another mirror... full of blackness and depression

Another mirror... and like a movie from the past, scenes of a young woman lost and alone, with a knife in one hand and bleeding from the other

Another mirror... and there she lay upon the surgery table, with tears in her eyes screaming "I just killed my baby!"

But, as Light stepped through this mirror, He was able to see the spiritual... and he saw the angels of God cradling the baby... its flesh had died, but its spirit lived on. Now free, it was given wings... and just before they all began flying upwards. The baby flew over to the mother and lightly kissed her upon the cheek, then whispered something into her ear. And while the angels flew away... there stood one remaining by her side. If it were not for this guardian angel, she wouldn't be here today.

Her grief and mourning soon turned into shame and guilt which then changed to anger and self hatred. It was in her weakest moment... when the door was opened to Misery. And once inside, Misery quickly locked the door behind her while chaining Passion somewhere into the darkness.

'No one could ever love you,' Izzy's voice could be heard just ahead...

Letting his presence be known... Light began walking closer while shining his light brighter...

'Beauty' he shouted

She quickly turned around startled...

'Who are... where did you... What are you doing here? And why do you call me Beauty?'

That was your name before you were ever born. I know you don't remember, but that is your name, Beauty'

'Don't listen to him,' Izzy hissed

'Beauty, I have come to free you from this prison. I come in the name of Love... for it is Love who sent me here'

"Liar!' Izzy screamed

'Beauty, you cannot live in the past any longer...'

'The past is what's made her what she is' Izzy argued... 'Without the past I would disappear!'

'Yes Misery... that's the whole point. I have come to free her of her haunted past... as well as you, Misery!'

It was Misery now, who was shaking in fear... as the light of Beauty's eyes began to shine...

"I'm ready... Beauty cried out... "I am so ready"

'Then smash these mirrors... and let's move on... it's time to step out of the past and into the present... and the future? It's time to redecorate this mind of yours with better memories... and to destroy those which have been distorted.

At first Beauty hesitated... partially because she had become attached to Misery, chained at the wrists

'Beauty... you need me' Izzy pleaded... don't do this... I am the only one who was there for you; I am the one who has kept you safe...'

'No Izzy... you have only kept me locked in this prison... and it was never about me, it was always about you.'

'But I love you....' Izzy whispered

'NO!!! Beauty screamed out... as she began smashing the mirrors and ripping down the pictures that Misery had put up. Distorted pictures that told her she was ugly, pictures that made her want to starve herself. Mirrors of broken shards, and shattered dreams. Mirrors which told her, you're better off dead...But with every broken mirror and picture, the chain attached to Misery began to weaken... as Izzy herself, began fading away. Until finally, the chain around her neck loosened and fell.

With one last mirror left... Beauty looked into the past one last time, and quietly whispered, 'I forgive you, all of you'

Smash! Crash!

Suddenly she was outside again... in the middle of a meadow of flowers and singing birds.

But now, even though free from her prison, free from her past... she was still unable to feel... still numb.
She could hear the birds and see the sun, but she could not feel them. She smiled, but there was no joy.

'Please don't leave me like this...' Beauty pleaded

'Of course not, sweet child... but I needed to remind you one last time, how it feels... not to feel. For there are many others out there, who are so cold and numb to this world... alone... You have been where they are; now you are called to lead them. You were not ready before... so I could not come, but I heard you calling me through the whispers of the night.'

'When... when did I call you?"

'I heard you when you were sleeping... for in was only in your dreams that you dared to cry out'

And with that, the angel placed his hand of light deep into the heart of Beauty... through the thorns and barbed wire and into the walls of ice.

Slowly... the walls came down... then suddenly the frozen waters melted and began flowing like a fountain... and peace began to overflow her eyes like a wild river, cascading over her cheeks and chin like a waterfall, forming droplets of rainbows as the rays of sun tore through them... Over her nose and lips they fell, a thunderstorm of tears showering the rose petals under her feet. The earth shook, as her walls began to crumble... walls of rejection, walls of betrayal, walls of regret, they all came smashing down as this flood destroyed all of the darkness... pain, misery, and guilt began washing away... until finally the skies of her mind cleared... And the fire in her heart burned once more.

And for the first time in many years, Beauty laughed.

And then... She Danced!

She danced onto the paths of the unknown, the roads of tomorrow... no longer looking behind, but forwards...

Have you ever seen Beauty dance?

sigh

It's breath taking... awe inspiring... like an angel, getting its first pair of wings.

listening to the wind

howl
she runs wildly
through the forest
rage upon her breath
breaking dead trees
the leaves fed her hunger
but her appetite could not be quenched
the pain that can never
be extinguished

the snow falls with her sadness
everything becomes a blizzard
so she runs
blindly
wildly
breaking everything in her path
she howls with madness
burying the snow angels
with her tears

In the mist, I listen to the wind howl as she runs wildly
through the forest breaking trees like hunger pains, the snow
falls with her sadness; so she runs and howls with madness -
burying the snow angels with her tears the emptiness screams,
but the memories will never surrender... so I close the door,
and hear the wind no more

tears and rain

with every drop of rain
a year of eternity fades away

our tears are the rain
from Life's thunderstorms

the pain in our hearts
is the strike of lightning

and our cry
the thunder which follows

Eric Shortridge is also the author of

Landon's Cry

Follow the Leader

The last words of a dying muse

available in paperback and digitally online
wherever great books are sold

Made in the USA
Coppell, TX
23 June 2022

79184977R00267